ON

QUINE

Lynn Hankinson Nelson
University of Missouri

Jack Nelson
University of Missouri

 **Wadsworth**
Thomson Learning.

Australia • Canada • Mexico • Singapore • Spain
United Kingdom • United States

Dedicated to

W. V. Quine

whose work has inspired and guided our work.

Printed in the United States of America
  2 3 4 5 6 7 03 02 01 00

For permission to use material from this text, contact us:
Web: www.thomsonrights.com
Fax: 1-800-730-2215
Phone: 1-800-730-2214

For more information, contact:
Wadsworth/Thomson Learning
10 Davis Drive
Belmont, CA 94002-3098
USA
http://www.wadsworth.com

ISBN: 0-534-57622-2

Contents

Preface

This monograph has been a labor of love. We have sought to explicate Quine in Quinean terms. We have not referenced secondary works on Quine, in the belief that Quine is his own best expositor and that what is needed, at most, is an overview of some of the main threads of the web that constitutes Quine's most serious going theory.

The most difficult parts of writing about Quine are starting and stopping to write. Both, we found, had to occur *in media res*, as there is no more a foundation to Quine's work than there is a foundation to science. Both are all of a piece.

We hope there is enough of the flavor of Quine in this volume to encourage students new to philosophy, and philosophers new to Quine, to delve more deeply into Quine's writings.

1
Introduction

I philosophize from the vantage point only of our own provincial conceptual scheme and scientific epoch, true; but I know no better.

– W. V. Quine[1]

Quine's Place in 20th Century Philosophy

W. V. Quine[2] is the Edgar Pierce Professor of Philosophy, Emeritus, at Harvard University. He was born in 1908 in Akron, Ohio. Quine attended Oberlin College as an undergraduate and earned his Ph.D. at Harvard, under C.I. Lewis. He is the preeminent American philosopher of the 20th century.

Quine falls within, and is influenced by, at least three intellectual traditions: the empiricist tradition of Locke, Hume, the Vienna Circle, Hempel, Nagel, Popper, and, most importantly, Carnap; the pragmatist tradition of James, Peirce, Dewey, and C.I. Lewis; and the tradition of modern mathematical logic, running from Russell and Whitehead through Gödel and Church. From the empiricist tradition comes Quine's life-long concern with explicating the relationship between experience and our best going theories of the world. From the pragmatist tradition comes his advocacy of holism and the tentativeness of all of science. From mathematical logic comes his commitment to extensionality and to Tarski's theory of truth. Quine is the clear heir to the empiricist program for which Carnap set the agenda in the 1930s, 40s and 50s. He is a product of this tradition, its own greatest critic, and, in the end, its ablest defender. His reconstruction of empiricism draws on the pragmatist tradition of Peirce, James, and Dewey, and his commitment to extensionality. He sees

1

philosophy as continuous with science and evolving from it, not prior to or transcendent of it.

The corpus of Quine's writings is the product of nearly 70 years of work. It is comprehensive, addressing most of the issues of interest to philosophers of the 20th century. The individual works of the corpus are interlocking, mutually supportive, and together more nearly consistent than it is reasonable to expect for a body of work that spans more than two-thirds of a century. While Quine's views have evolved over the decades, there has been no radical change in direction or commitment. Every sentence of every article and every book is carefully crafted, for both content and style.

Quine is a philosophers' philosopher. He writes for, and is read primarily by, other philosophers. He has laid out a view of what philosophy is and how it should be done: philosophy is an extension of science (it is science gone self-conscious), and it is to be done using the methods of inquiry and standards of evidence of science itself, and drawing upon the findings of science. Philosophical theories, like theories of science, are tested against the world, that is, by how well they explain and predict experience. There is no higher standard.

Quine holds that philosophy of science is philosophy enough (1966h, 149). It is therefore no surprise that he has not worked extensively in the area of value theory (aesthetics, ethics, action theory). But his notion of science is a broad one, encompassing all of our serious theories about the world, including ourselves, and our place in the world. Understanding science– understanding how we come to formulate, revise, accept, and reject theories– is what philosophy (of science) is about. It is the endeavor of the reflective scientist and layperson as well as of the professional philosopher. It is philosophy enough because speculations going beyond science also go beyond evidence, and therefore beyond sense.

Quine is an empiricist, which is to say he believes that whatever support science has rests ultimately on sensory experiences, and that it is, in the end, those experiences that provide whatever empirical content our theories have. The only sense of "meaning" that makes sense to Quine is that of empirical content as it is derived from sensory experience.

Quine has a theory of language acquisition and as a logician he cares deeply about the logical relations among sentences and sets of sentences. He is interested in linguistics as an empirical discipline and he is interested in the history of languages and speaks and writes in multiple languages. But he does not have a theory of "meaning"–a semantical theory that is distinct from and more than a recognition of the logical relations among sentences and sets of sentences, a behaviorist analysis of language learning and use,[3] a recognition of the importance and power of contextual definition, and an

2

account of sense experience as the basis of all empirical content. Quine does have a theory of truth, Tarski's, but his primary concern has been evidence, not truth, and one of his life's projects has been explicating how sense experience provides the empirical content for all of our theories, however abstract.

Quine has set the agenda for British-American, and perhaps for all of philosophy, from about 1950 through at least the 1980s. Philosophers working during that period, on any of the many topics Quine has touched upon, dared ignore Quine's views only at their own peril. Those philosophers who cling firmly to theories of language that countenance talk of the meaning of individual words and sentences feel obliged to offer a response to Quine's rejection of the analytic/synthetic distinction and of the notion that meaning is something distinct from empirical content. Those who hold some form of correspondence theory of truth and/or a commitment to the reality of macro, micro, or atomic or subatomic objects independent of the conceptual scheme we weave, must address Quine's arguments for holism and pragmatism. Those committed to modal logic need to respond to Quine's dismissal of that subject as fundamentally confused.

Quintessentially Quine

Quine has published two autobiographies, a relatively brief one in *The Philosophy of W.V. Quine*, edited by Hahn and Schilpp, and an extensive one, *The Time of My Life*, published by MIT Press. We commend both to those who want a fuller sense of Quine's passage through the years and countries of the 20th century.

The list of Quine's doctoral students includes Donald Davidson, Hugues Leblanc, William Craig, Hao Wang, Burton Dreben, and Dagfinn Føllesdal. Though Quine clearly always preferred research to teaching,[4] or at least to undergraduate teaching, his graduate students are clearly devoted to him. Administrative duties had even less appeal than classroom teaching. He chaired the Harvard philosophy department only once, and describes it as "a chore of four years or so that was passed around" (1985, 228).[5]

As topics for polite conversation Quine prefers geography and languages to philosophy. (Quine's works have been widely translated. By his own account, there are six foreign languages in which he is competent to check the translations (1985, 422)). One of us asked Quine how many countries he had not been to. He gave an answer and launched into an explanation of how this number was calculated, based on recent changes in national boundaries. Douglas Boynton Quine, Quine's son, maintains a web page devoted to his father.[6] The web page includes a list of countries Quine has visited (118), a list of additional countries Quine has not visited but has "flown over" (19), and a list of countries he has neither visited nor flown over, but has "seen from the side as passing by" (8).

Most philosophers who have met or corresponded with Quine have fond memories of those interactions that are "typically Quine." Jack Nelson remembers trying to teach Quine to ride a surfboard in 1971. Lynn Hankinson Nelson remembers being embarrassed, when Quine asked her whether she and Jack spoke Swedish at home. She admitted she did not, but let Quine think, erroneously, that Jack did. In a closing note to a letter about a work in progress by Jack Nelson, Quine congratulated him for having "thrown off the administrative yoke," which he had not. One of our fondest memories of Quine is watching him and his wife, Marjorie Boynton Quine, stroll the halls of a conference held at Rutgers in the mid 80s, hand in hand.

Quine goes out of his way to be encouraging to new philosophers who are interested in his work, and is generally very patient with their attempts to find flaws in his arguments. One of us witnessed a young philosopher try to defend the analytic/synthetic distinction by appeal to the Kantian notion of meaning inclusion. Quine sat quietly through the paper and the discussion that followed. When asked for his own view of the paper, instead of pointing out that the author had given no account whatsoever of how meanings were to be identified and meaning inclusion determined, Quine simply suggested that we had worked hard enough for one day and should adjourn for a drink.

Quine's criticisms of other philosophers, even when he vehemently disagrees with them, are nearly approbatory. John Austin's and Quine's approaches to philosophy have almost nothing in common. But in the closing comments of his paper "On Austin's Method" Quine writes only:

> Historians of science tell us that science forges ahead not by an indiscriminate Baconian inductivism but by pursuing preconceptions, even mistaken ones. I see in Austin's work this kind of progress (1981f, 91).

Quine is an extensionalist; he thinks modal logic rests on a serious, and near obvious, confusion. Yet in his response to Saul Kripke, the 20th century's greatest advocate of modal logic, Quine writes:

> The notion of possible worlds did indeed contribute to the semantics of modal logic, and it behooves us to recognize the nature of its contribution: it led to Kripke's precocious and significant theory of models of modal logic. Models afford consistency proofs; also they have heuristic value; but they do not constitute explication...I can read Kripke gratefully as abetting my effort to show what a tangled web the modalist weaves (1981g, 173-174).

4

Quine cares about style, about the elegance of his writing, about crafting just the right "turn of phrase."[7] Although Quine does not write "for" the non-philosopher, his writings will strike almost every reader as clearer, more straightforward, and more expertly crafted by literary standards, than those of any other 20th century philosopher. He uses simple, clear, elegant sentences. They are more often short than long, more often in the active than in the passive voce. Quine rarely uses strung together dependent clauses or long parenthetical remarks. His expressed preference for desert landscapes (1963a, 4) is a metaphor for his view of the entire world, and he takes language to be a part of the world.

As noted above, Quine's interests extend beyond philosophy to include languages and geography. His review of *The Times Atlas of the World* (1981h, 199) opens with this wonderful sentence:

> This is a sturdy twelve-pounder and stands a foot and a half high...

and continues with

> Western Europe begins with a double page of Iceland, just Iceland, a full twenty inches from cape to cape, all delicately tinted green and tan for elevations and white for glaciers and surrounded by the blue sea. Other tastefully sea-girt subjects of great two-page spreads are New Guinea, Ireland, northern Scotland...

Quine enjoys structuring his papers around quasi-literary devices. In "Grades of Theoreticity," he accumulates ironies (six in all); in "Five Milestones of Empiricism" the unifying theme is, obviously, milestones. In "Posits and Reality" it is the ways in which different kinds of posits are each fundamental in their own way. In "Two Dogmas of Empiricism" Quine repeatedly finds that proffered accounts of problematic philosophical notions turn out to be "as much in need of clarification" as is the notion being explicated. In the title essay of *Ways of Paradox*, Quine collects, of course, paradoxes (and antinomies).

Before turning to Quine's specific views we cannot resist repeating here some of our favorite passages from Quine's works:

> We sit and think, but do we sit and believe? The White Queen, indeed, professed to do so. "When I was your age, I always did it for half-an-hour a day. Why, sometimes I've believed as many as six impossible things before breakfast." But it will be agreed that the White Queen was atypical (1987a, 19).

> A curious thing about the ontological problem is its simplicity. It can be put in three Anglo-Saxon monosyllables: 'What is there?' It can be answered, moreover, in a word 'Everything' (1963a, 1).

Our argument is not flatly circular, but something like it. It has the form, figuratively speaking, of a closed curve in space (1963b, 30).

Or better still, we might just stop tugging at our bootstraps altogether (1963b, 36; said about attempts to specify the analytic statements of a formal language).

Boundaries between disciplines are useful for deans and librarians, but let us not overestimate them–the boundaries (1966c, 56).

I am a physical object sitting in a physical world. Some of the forces of this physical world impinge on my surface. Light rays strike my retinas; molecules bombard my eardrums and fingertips. I strike back, emanating concentric air waves. These waves take the form of a torrent of discourse about tables, people, molecules, light rays, retinas, air waves, prime numbers, infinite classes, joy and sorrow, good and evil" (1966f, 215).

For me then the problem of induction is a problem about the world: a problem of how we, as we now are (by our present scientific lights), in a world we never made, should stand better than random or coin-tossing chance of coming out right when we predict by inductions which are based on our innate, scientifically unjustified similarity standard. Darwin's natural selection is a plausible partial explanation (1969d, 127).

Our talk of external things, our very notion of things, is just a conceptual apparatus that helps us to foresee and control the triggering of our sensory receptors in the light of previous triggering of our sensory receptors. The triggering, first and last, is all we have to go on (1981a, 1).

...science is a conceptual bridge of our own making, linking sensory stimulation to sensory stimulation; there is no extrasensory perception (1981a, 2).

Quine's Project

David Hume held that there are two kinds of truths, those resting on the "relations of [among] ideas" and those resting on "matters of fact." An alleged example of the former is "A pentagon has more sides than a square," one of the latter is "MacArthur left Corregidor by PT boat." The former is, or so the story goes, made true by the relations among the "meanings" of 'pentagon', 'square', 'more', 'side', and so on. Given that these terms mean what they do, it could not but be true. Its truth is therefore certain, but also uninformative—it tells us nothing we did not know already by knowing the meaning of the constituent terms. But "MacArthur left Corregidor by PT boat" is otherwise. To know of MacArthur's leaving Corregidor is to know a bit of history, an event that happened when and as it did, but might not have happened or might have happened differently.

By dividing truths into these two kinds, known later as "analytic" truths and "synthetic" truths, Hume set a new standard for intellectual respectability and set an agenda for future empiricists. For Hume's successors, reasoning concerning analytic statements was to yield the truths of logic and mathematics. Synthetic truths were to be the domain and product of science. Everything else is nonsense. The new standard is embodied in the famous last paragraph of Hume's *An Enquiry Concerning Human Understanding.*

> When we run over libraries, persuaded of these principles, what havoc must we make? If we take in our hand any volume, of divinity or school metaphysics, for instance; let us ask, Does it contain any abstract reasoning concerning quantity or number? No. Does it contain any experimental reasoning concerning matter of fact and existence? No. Commit it then to the flames: for it can contain nothing but sophistry and illusion (Hume, 1902, 165).

By limiting meaningful claims to matters of fact and relations of ideas Hume thought he had effectively dispensed not only with doctrines of secret powers (*e.g.*, of causation) and metaphysical doctrines of self and substances, but also with all of religion save natural religion (what is now called 'natural theology', which he demolished in his *Dialogues Concerning Natural Religion*).

The agenda Hume set for future empiricists is this: show how all claims we want to hold as meaningful—as either true or false—derive either from relations of ideas or matters of fact. In the two centuries following Hume's death philosophers and mathematicians labored to complete Hume's agenda. On the "relations of ideas" side they sought to show that all of logic and mathematics consists of analytic truths.[8]

The empiricist part of Hume's agenda—that of showing that all synthetic truths are empirical claims whose support rests ultimately on sense experience—was pursued assiduously by members of the Vienna Circle, and, after it dispersed, by such philosophers as Carl Hempel, Ernst Nagel, Karl Popper, and, most importantly (at least in Quine's intellectual development), Rudolf Carnap. The tradition within which they worked, from the 1930s through the 1960s, became known as the "logico-empiricist" tradition, because they, like Hume, thought every truth could be accounted for either on grounds of logic (relations of ideas) or of sensory experience (matters of fact). In broad strokes they sought to develop a coherent account of empirical knowledge that identified the meaning of a sentence with the method or process or content of the procedure used to verify (or reject) the sentence, and that revealed how all empirical knowledge rests, in the end, on sensory experiences. (Karl Popper, of course, rejected verificationism for falsificationism, something of its mirror twin).

The driving force behind this endeavor was two-fold. First, it was assumed that all we initially know is what is immediately presented to us through our senses, and hence that claims that go beyond this immediate presentation need to be justified by or replaced with claims about sense experience. Second, it was assumed that sentences reporting sensory experience, or the sensory experiences themselves, are cognitively privileged–they are unmediated, and because they are, they offer no room for error. Given these two assumptions, it follows that if we can either reduce all the empirical claims we care about to sensory experiences or claims about them, or alternatively replace those claims with claims about sensory experiences, we will have eliminated the possibility of error, will have placed science on a firm foundation, and will have decisively refuted the skeptic.[9] Carnap's approach was perhaps the most formal. He attempted, in his *Der logische Aufbau der Welt*, to develop a "language" of sensory experience that in theory could supplant our ordinary language. In Quine's words, the project of the *Aufbau* was that of "specifying a sense-datum language and showing how to translate the rest of significant discourse, statement by statement, into it" (1963b, 39).

Although Quine studied under Carnap in Prague in 1933 and continued to be influenced by him at least through the 1950s, he became uneasy with the Humean agenda as early as 1936, when "Truth by Convention" appeared. In that article Quine does not argue that mathematics is not reducible to logic ("There is no need here to adopt a final stand in the matter" (80)). But he does argue that logic itself cannot be construed as true by definition:

> But if we are to construe logic also as true by convention, we must rest logic ultimately upon some manner of convention other than definition: for it was noted earlier that definitions are available only for transforming truths, not for founding them (1966d, 81).

Quine next explores whether various other conventions might be the basis for the truths of logic and mathematics. He concludes that it is unlikely, showing that logic itself is needed to explicate both logic and mathematics.

Definitions are taken by most philosophers to be one kind of analytic truth. "Truth by Convention" is an important article because it shows that if logic and mathematics consist, in the end, of analytic truths, those truths cannot be definitional truths. Later, in "Two Dogmas of Empiricism," Quine argues that other varieties of and explanations of analyticity fail, leaving no room for giving an account of mathematical truths and logical truths distinct from that given for the truths of science generally.

In "Truth by Convention" Quine even hints of his later view of why we tend to see the truths of mathematics and logic as having a special status, *e.g.*, being analytic or true by convention. They have no such special status, but they do permeate all of science, and therefore changes to them would have implications for every part of science. They are, therefore, the "statements which we choose to surrender last, if at all, in the course of revamping our sciences in the face of new discoveries" (1966d, 95). We invent doctrines of analyticity and truth by convention to explain why we are reluctant to give up or modify the claims of mathematics and logic. That is, it is our unwillingness to abandon claims of mathematics and logic that explains why we think they must be true in some special way, rather than their being true by in some special way that explains why we are unwilling to abandon them. There is, as we will subsequently see, more than a little of Quine's later holism here.

Thus as early as 1936 Quine set the stage for his subsequent rejection of the analytic/synthetic distinction in "Two Dogmas of Empiricism." We will later review the arguments of that article. Here we note that the agenda that is to occupy Quine for the rest of his career is already laid out, in broad strokes, in "Truth by Convention." He is committed to maintaining both the truth and the importance of the claims of logic and mathematics,[10] and he is unable to avail himself of the Humean defense of these disciplines (that they rest on relations of ideas).

Quine is also committed to empiricism. His challenge is to be able to specify the way in which experience bears on the claims of science without presupposing the analytic/synthetic distinction and in a way that explains why we are so reluctant to consider abandoning any of the claims of logic and mathematics. Quine's answer is twofold: holism, a doctrine to which we will subsequently devote considerable space, and an evolving account of sense experience. Here we give a broad sketch.

Science, including anatomy, physiology, optics, audiology, as well as physics, chemistry and psychology (and not forgetting mathematics and logic) gives us a theory of the world. According to this theory the world includes gross physical objects (stars, planets, tables, chairs, people) as well as molecular, atomic, and subatomic particles, and sets of these objects. This is a picture we have built for ourselves over time. There are tensions in the theory (how can something as solid as a desk "really" be a swarm of vibrating molecules? (1966g, 233)), and attempts to explain those tensions. This theory also tells us that we come to know about the world through our sense receptors. Telepathy and extrasensory perception don't work. Neither does *a priori* reasoning about what the world must be like. Our cognition of the world starts, science tells us, through firings of our sensory receptors. Science also tells us that we are not aware of these firings *per se*. There is no phenomenology of experience that correlates with the firings of sensory receptors, yet the firings are real and discoverable–by the normal methods of science (empirical psychology, physiology, anatomy).

The firings of sensory receptors are physiological events, not sentences (and therefore not candidates for truth or falsity) and not (at least in the first instance) phenomena of which we are aware. They are our only connection to the "external" world; they provide the only evidence we have for our theories. But they are not foundational in the sense of being "indubitable" or "self-evident." Nor is our knowledge of them prior to science. Rather it is through science that we know of them.

> It remains a fact, a fact of science itself, that science is a conceptual bridge of our own making, linking sensory stimulation to sensory stimulation; there is no extrasensory perception (1981a, 2).

The bridge we, as a species, have built was formed first, historically speaking, of enduring middle-sized objects and later of molecules, atoms, sub-atomic particles, and sets. How we, as individuals, come to accept this bridge is a story developmental psychology has to tell, a story Quine speculates about in several of his works. How we as a species or as a community of inquirers have built this bridge is a story for the history of science and naturalized epistemology to tell.

A few brief notes about terminology are in order.

Quine tends to use the term 'statement' where others would use 'sentence' or 'indicative sentence'. By 'statement' Quine does not mean some non-linguistic entity that is the meaning of a sentence as asserted on a particular occasion–he simply means 'indicative sentence'. We tend to use 'statement' in discussing those articles in which Quine favors that term, and for us, as for Quine, it means only 'indicative sentence'. When we do use 'sentence' we generally mean 'indicative sentence'. Quine has always preferred the term 'class' to the term 'set'. We use 'set' because it has become the standard.

Theories figure prominently in Quine's writings–it is theories rather than individual sentences that "confront the tribunal of experience." It is theories that carry ontological commitment. But what is a theory? Quine sidesteps this issue by suggesting that we center our attention on "the sentences that express them [theories]."

> There will be no need to decide what a theory is or when to regard two sets of sentences as formulations of the same theory; we can just talk of the theory formulations as such (1981b, 24).

Theory formulations are sets of sentences. This move from theories to theory formulations has an additional advantage. Since theory formulations just are sets of sentences there are, of course, infinitely many theory formulations. It follows that the question "How plausible does a view have to be to count as a scientific theory?" is a non-starter. If the view is expressible by a set of sentences, then it has a theory formulation and counts as a theory. The above question is then replaced with "How do we determine whether this theory [theory formulation] is better than that theory [theory formulation]?" And it is in many ways easier to specify what makes one theory better than another than it is to define a plausibility threshold such that only views meeting that threshold count as theories at all.

Quine consistently uses masculine pronouns as if they were generic, and uses 'mankind' and 'man' to refer to humanity. This, we submit, reflects the accepted usage of the time period within which many of the articles we quote from were written. Although we don't think there is, in fact, a generic sense to 'he', 'man', and 'mankind' (or that declaring them to be generic can make them so), we have opted not to add 'sic' each time these and similar terms occur in a passage we quote.

Lastly, we noted above that Quine does have a theory of truth, Tarski's. We will not have room in this volume to discuss a variety of topics Quine has dealt with, including his use of Tarski's theory of truth. Suffice it to say here that Tarski's theory of truth makes truth immanent, not transcendent, and it applies equally (even if equally uninformatively) to the truths of logic and mathematics, and to the truths of empirical science. The paradigm usually used to illustrate Tarski's theory is the following account of the truth of 'Snow is white':

> 'Snow is white' is true if and only if snow is white.

Apparently only slightly less trivial is

> 'Snow is white and cold' is true if and only if snow is white and snow is cold.

On Tarski's account, truth is immanent because truth is explained relative to, and using expressions of, the language in question. No reference is made to a world/language match or correspondence or other alleged metaphysical reality. Tarski's theory has also been termed the "disappearance" theory of truth because once understood it serves to emphasize that in science, and the philosophy of science, the hard work concerns not truth but evidence.

Endnotes

[1] "Speaking of Objects," 25.

[2] In his earlier works, through at least *From a Logical Point of View* and *Methods of Logic* Quine signed his name as 'Willard Van Orman Quine', and was frequently referred to as 'W.V.O. Quine'. Subsequently he switched to 'W.V. Quine', and is known to his friends as 'Van'.

[3] In his reply to Harman in *Words and Objections* Quine writes "I am not sure what philosophical behaviorism involves, but I do consider myself as behavioristic as anyone in his right mind could be" (Davidson, 1969, 296).

[4] Quine only taught Hume once, and notes in *The Time of My Life* that "by the end of the course my lecture notes were full and ready for a repeat performance in another year, but I could not bear to offer the course again. Determining what Hume thought and imparting it to my students was less appealing than determining the truth and imparting that" (1985, 194).

[5] All references are to works by W.V. Quine unless otherwise indicated.

[6] The address of the web site is http://www.triskelion-ltd.com/drquine/wv-quine.html.

[7] Quine is fond of the *bon mot*. But he does note in his Hahn and Schilpp autobiography that while "It is a pleasure to hit upon a clever and amusing way of making some point that wanted making," when it comes to deciding between accuracy or clarity and cleverness, he opts for the former, unless the topic is, *e.g.*, "one of my fun reviews for the *New York Review of Books*," where he is "apt to keep the *bon mot*." Quine remarks "Here I see a boundary mark between *belles lettres* and science" (1987b, 46).

[8] It was hoped that, for mathematics and logic, truth could be identified with provability. That is, a statement of mathematics or logic would be true if and only if it were a theorem in an appropriate formal system. This project, pursued by Hilbert in the first decades of the 20th century, came to a halt when Kurt Gödel proved, in 1931, that truth and provability cannot be identified, even for arithmetic truths. The substance of Gödel's result is, in Quine's words,

> that no deductive system, with axioms however arbitrary, is capable of embracing among its theorems all the truths of the elementary arithmetic of positive integers unless it discredits itself by letting slip some of the

falsehoods too. Gödel showed how, for any given deductive system, he could construct a sentence of elementary number theory that would be true if and only if not provable in that system (1966a, 18-19).

Although Hilbert's project was abandoned, efforts continued to show that logical truths and mathematical truths are different in kind from empirical truths, *e.g.*, they are true by definition or by convention.

[9] Readers may notice a tension here. Science is by its very nature public, an enterprise conducted within a community of investigators sharing (or disputing) assumptions, techniques, theories. Sensory experience is, again by its very nature, private, perhaps even incommunicable. The attempt to reduce science to, or replace it with, claims about sense experience is, therefore, on the face of it implausible if not a non-starter. It is part of Quine's genius that he not only saw this tension but also took as his challenge the relating of science to sense experience while not abandoning the public for the private, the communicable and testable for the unstructured and incommunicable fleeting present of sensory experience.

[10] "Irrefragability, thy name is mathematics" (1966b, 24).

2
All the Evidence There Is

The proper role of experience or surface irritation is as a basis not for truth but for warranted belief... Empiricism as a theory of truth thereupon goes by the board, and good riddance. As a theory of evidence, however, empiricism remains with us.

– W.V. Quine[1]

The Cardinal Tenets of Empiricism

The "cardinal tenets of empiricism," Quine maintains in "Epistemology Naturalized," are two.

> The first is that whatever evidence there is for science is sensory evidence. The other... is that all inculcation of meanings of words must rest ultimately on sensory evidence (75).

These tenets mark empiricism as a theory of evidence (rather than a theory of truth), and distinguish it from other theories of evidence.[2]

As just stated, these tenets are admittedly somewhat cryptic. Locke and Hume would probably have accepted them. Locke took ideas, Hume impressions (of which ideas are copies), to constitute sensory experience and sensory evidence, and identified meaning with ideas–mental objects of which we are directly aware. Quine does neither. That is, he assumes neither that sensory experience–which constitutes all the evidence there is–is something mental, nor that we are aware of it. Nor does he assume that empirical meaning consists of ideas. What Quine does take to constitute sensory evidence, and to what he attributes empirical meaning, are not revealed by these tenets. Nor do these tenets reveal how sensory evidence gets connected with the theories we weave from it, be they theories of evolutionary biology

14

or high-energy physics or of the middle sized objects we take to surround us. These are complicated topics, topics to which Quine has returned again and again over the past seven decades. Over that period Quine has consistently explicated empirical meaning or content in the terms of sensory experience, and sensory experience as the "stimulation of sensory receptors," the "firings of our sensory receptors," and most recently as the "triggerings of exteroceptors." Quine's notion of sensory experience is thus physicalist, not phenomenological, and experience so understood is the basis for whatever empirical content sentences and theories have. The details of these positions, and their implications, will concern us in the chapters that follow. Here, we paint, in broad strokes, the general outlines of Quinean empiricism.

A persistent theme in Quine's writings is that we work within and contribute to the traditions of inquiry we inherit, without benefit of foundations or Archimedean standpoints. "Analyze theory building as we may," Quine notes in Word and Object, "we always begin in the middle" (4). This view of science and the philosophy of science as going concerns, enterprises without foundations, extends to the core tenets of empiricism. These, Quine maintains, are not first principles, coming before science. They are instead findings of science. It is on the basis of our best going theories "that we come to appreciate that the world can be evidenced only through stimulation of our senses" (1966g, 239), and in what that stimulation consists (the triggerings of exteroceptors).

> The crucial insight of empiricism is that any evidence for science has its end points in the senses. This insight remains valid, but it is an insight which comes after physics, physiology, and psychology, not before (1966e, 212).

We are not, contrary to what Locke and Hume assumed, directly aware of our sensory experiences. As Quine quips in "On the Very Idea of a Third Dogma," "few people, statistically speaking, know about their nerve endings" (40). We are aware of bodies, big and small; of words and discourse, our own and others; of events, major and minor; of theories, more and less esoteric, and so forth. What, then, connects all of this with the physiological processes of which we are not aware but that nonetheless provide all the evidence we have for bodies, words, events and so forth?

The answer, Quine again suggests, will be provided by science itself. The findings of science explain (or can be expected to eventually explain) how our senses work and what kinds of information they yield, as well as how language is learned and used. It is here that Quine's twin

15

theses of naturalism and holism come together. Naturalism is the thesis that we can do no better than to accept what science tells us about sense perception, language learning, and theory formation. Holism is the story of how science works, of how we build, modify, and occasionally reject theories using our best going theories and the evidence science tells us we get from our senses. These theses, summarized below, will receive extended treatment in subsequent chapters.

It is doubtful that Quine ever thought empiricism could be a foundationalist project–finding in sense experience, construed as something of which we are (or can become) immediately aware, the building blocks out of which all of science can be reconstructed without using the findings and tools of science. If he did, he had clearly given up that project by the time he wrote "Two Dogmas of Empiricism" (1953), and probably by the time he wrote "Truth by Convention" (1936). In *Word and Object*, Quine's rejection of the foundationalist project is full blown:

> Impressed with the fact that we know external things only mediately through our senses, philosophers from Berkeley onward have undertaken to strip away the physicalistic conjectures and bare the sense data. Yet even as we try to recapture the data, in all their innocence of interpretation, we find ourselves depending upon sidelong glances into natural science... the trouble is that immediate experience simply will not, of itself, cohere as an autonomous domain. References to physical things are largely what hold it together. These references are not just inessential vestiges of the initially intersubjective character of language, capable of being weeded out by devising an artificially subjective language for sense data. Rather they give us our main continuing access to past sense data themselves; for past sense data are mostly gone for good except as commemorated in physical posits... Conceptualization on any considerable scale is inseparable from language, and our ordinary language of physical things is about as basic as language gets (1960, 1-3).

Quine is abandoning not only the foundationalist project of grounding science in immediately given and purportedly error-free sense data. He is also abandoning the view implicit in foundationalism that each of us, individually and privately, constructs the world out of our own sense experiences. Conceptualization is necessary for coherent experience, language is necessary for conceptualization, and language is public. These positions, too, will be considered in detail in later chapters.

16

Recall that there are two "cardinal tenets of empiricism": "Whatever evidence there *is* for science *is* sensory evidence" and "All inculcation of meanings of words must rest ultimately on sensory evidence." We now have a fair understanding of Quine's notion of sensory experience (that it is, in the end, the triggerings of exteroceptors), although more remains to be said. We have not yet had much to say about the "inculcation of meanings of words." We have noted that Quine does not take the meanings of words to be mental entities (e.g., ideas). Nor does he take the meanings of sentences to be non-physical entities (for example, propositions) that are "expressed by" sentences. Rather, the only notion of meaning Quine finds intelligible is that of *empirical meaning or content*. It is linguistic entities that have empirical meaning or content, and the empirical meaning they have is, in the end, constituted by the triggerings of exteroceptors. The critical question, then, is this: how are the physiological processes that constitute experience, and thus empirical content, connected to the theories we build (to *what* bits or chunks of language does empirical meaning attach, and *how* does it so attach)?

"Five Milestones of Empiricism"

In "Five Milestones of Empiricism," Quine addresses these issues, although only in broad strokes. His view concerning the bearers of empirical meaning or content is that, apart from a narrowly defined class of sentences (observation sentences and their kin), empirical meaning or content attaches only to sets of sentences, *i.e.*, to theories. This is Quine's thesis of holism, and one issue for it is whether empirical content attaches only to the whole of science, broadly construed, or whether less than all encompassing bodies of theory are large enough to have empirical content. The first three of the advances or milestones in empiricism Quine speaks of in this essay mark the path to holism.

The path begins with Locke's ideas, but John Horne Tooke planted the first milestone when he switched the focus of empiricism from ideas to words:

> British empiricism was dedicated to the proposition that only sense makes sense. Ideas were acceptable only if based on sense impressions. But Tooke appreciated that the *idea* idea itself measures up poorly to empiricist standards (68.)

Tooke's insight was, in Quine's terms, that "words [not ideas] make sense only insofar as they are definable in sensory terms" (68.) One reason this is a milestone is that words, unlike ideas, are public.

17

Another is that ideas, construed as mental entities, lack clear identity conditions. While Quine is not a materialist (he countenances numbers and sets), he will not countenance entities without identities, entities for which it is impossible to say when we have the same, as opposed to another, entity of the sort in question. The identity conditions for mental entities are far from clear. Those for words are not as unclear, and we can always fall back on "the printer's use of spaces" (1960,13) as determining wordhood.

It is interesting to compare Quine's attitude towards sensory experience with his attitude towards mental entities, specifically ideas. The identity conditions for sensory experiences are far from clear, yet Quine needs a notion of sensory experience–it is part and parcel of empiricism. So he works to clean it up, and ends up with this:

> By the stimulation undergone by a subject on a given occasion I just mean the temporally ordered set of all those of his exteroceptors that are triggered on that occasion (1990b, 2).

This is an arcane, but clear notion. Quine does not work to clean up the idea idea, or other mental concepts. If empiricism needed ideas, or a cleaned up version of them, he might work to clean them up; but empiricism does not and he does not.

For Quine, the second milestone of empiricism is the shift from viewing terms (words) as those things which have "separable bundles of observable and testable consequences" (1981e, 70), *i.e.,* as have empirical meaning or content, to recognizing whole sentences as the bearers of such meaning or content. Quine attributes this shift to Bentham's theory of contextual definition, which recognized that the meaning of words is relative to their role in sentences. This shift, Quine maintains was no less of a "shift in center" for empiricism than the Copernican revolution was for physics (1981e, 69), and its consequences were substantial. The focus on sentences facilitated some of the more significant developments in twentieth century philosophy of science: Tarski's theory of truth, Hempel's and Nagel's model of explanation, models of the logic of theories and of justification, and work to develop first order quantification as the canonical form for science. More generally, Quine notes, the shift from terms to sentences changed epistemology from "a critique... primarily of concepts" to a critique "of truths and beliefs" (1981e, 70).

The third milestone of empiricism on Quine's list is the shift from sentences to system of sentences as the loci of empirical meaning or content, *i.e.,* the shift to holism. Quine is, of course, the architect and prime mover behind this shift. The shift is made most explicitly in

"Two Dogmas of Empiricism," where Quine rejects the verificationist principle that there is, for each meaningful sentence, a determinate list of stimulus conditions from which the sentence is derived or derivable, or on the basis of which it is verified. With this move from sentences to sets of sentences "we cease to demand or expect of a scientific sentence that it have its own separable empirical meaning" (1981e, 71). In "Two Dogmas" Quine suggests that "The unit of empirical significance is the whole of science" (42).

In *Word and Object*, Quine uses the metaphor of an arch to explicate the sharing of empirical content or meaning, and thus of empirical support, among the sentences of all seriously maintained theories.

> Theory may be deliberate, as in a chapter on chemistry, or it may be second nature, as is the immemorial doctrine of ordinary enduring middle-sized objects. In either case, theory causes a sharing, by sentences, of sensory supports. In an arch, an overhead block is supported immediately by other overhead blocks, and ultimately by all the base blocks collectively and none individually; and so it is with sentences, when theoretically fitted...
>
> What comes of the association of sentences with sentences is a vast verbal structure which, primarily as a whole, is multifariously linked to non-verbal stimulation. (11-12).

Holism is a significant and controversial thesis, one we will subsequently discuss in considerable detail. We here note that it undermines a cherished notion of science, that of the crucial experiment–an experiment that can decisively confirm or disconfirm an hypothesis or theory.

> ...the total field [all of science] is so underdetermined by its boundary conditions, experience, that there is much latitude of choice as to what statements to reevaluate in the light of any single contrary experience. No particular experiences are linked with any particular statements in the interior of the field, except indirectly through considerations of equilibrium affecting the field as a whole (1963b, 42-43).

The fourth milestone of empiricism, "methodological monism," follows from the third and the rejection of the analytic/synthetic distinction. Methodological monism is simply the thesis that holism applies, alike, to all sentences, including those of mathematics and logic. In "Two Dogmas," Quine puts the thesis this way:

> My present suggestion is that it is nonsense, and the root of much nonsense, to speak of a linguistic component and a factual component in the truth of any individual statement. Taken collectively, science has its double dependence upon language and experience; but this duality is not significantly traceable into the statements of science taken one by one (42).

In "Five Milestones," Quine relates the abandonment of the analytic/synthetic distinction directly to the shift to holism.

> The organizing role that was supposedly the role of analytic sentences is now seen as shared by sentences generally, and the empirical content that was supposedly peculiar to synthetic sentences is now seen as diffused through the system (72).

Quine's fifth milestone of empiricism is "epistemological naturalism." It, too, is a milestone for which he is responsible. Quine argues that having given up both the view that most sentences have isolatable empirical content and the analytic/synthetic distinction, one further aspect of traditional and positivist empiricism must be abandoned: "the goal of a first philosophy" (1981e, 72), the vision of the philosophy of science (or epistemology) as an enterprise that will identify "extra-scientific foundations" for science and, in so doing, justify or vindicate science. The philosophy of science, Quine maintains, should be recognized and pursued as part of the overall enterprise of science.

In "Epistemology Naturalized," Quine relates the naturalized epistemology he advocates to developments we have outlined in this chapter, namely the shift to holism and the demise of foundationalism.

> Philosophers have rightly despaired of translating everything into observational and logico-mathematical terms... and the impossibility of that sort of epistemological reduction dissipated the last advantage that rational reconstruction seemed to have over psychology... (83).

In "Five Milestones," Quine attributes the shift to naturalism to "two sources, both negative" (72). These are the failure of foundationalism and an "unregenerate realism." The "scientific epistemologist" who makes free use of the knowledge science provides to gain insight into "how we human animals... have managed to arrive at science from such limited information" is no longer interested in answering the skeptic (hence, Quine's description of this source as "negative"); this epistemologist, like the natural scientist, "has never felt any qualms beyond the negotiable uncertainties internal to science"

(72).

We devote a later chapter to naturalized epistemology. Here we remind readers that naturalism extends to Quine's understanding of the core tenets of empiricism. Quine maintains that these tenets are implications of science–that we (unabashedly) use the information the sciences provide as evidence of the nature of evidence.

We now have an overview of Quine's view of the progress of empiricism. With the exception of observation sentences and their kin (these will be considered in later chapters), it is systems of sentences–the theories that constitute the whole of science or some large part of it–that have empirical content or meaning. Both words and sentences, as bearers of empirical meaning, have gone by the way. Experience remains at the heart of the matter, but it is demystified as the triggerings of exteroceptors. The empiricist tenet that all the evidence there is is provided by our senses, remains. But it is no longer viewed as a "first principle" of a "first science." It is taken, instead, as a fact of science itself.

Endnotes

[1] "On the Very Idea of a Third Dogma," 39.

[2] In a number of places, Quine maintains that empiricism is a theory of evidence, not of truth, and we explore this more fully in later chapters. Quine's "On the Very Idea of a Third Dogma" contains one of the clearest explanations of why this is so.

3
Two Dogmas

Our argument is not flatly circular, but something like it. It has the
form, figuratively speaking, of a closed curve in space.

– W.V. Quine[1]

Quine published "Two Dogmas of Empiricism" in 1953 as the
second of nine essays in *From a Logical Point of View*. (It first
appeared in print in the *Philosophical Review*, in 1951). In it Quine
rejects outright the analytic/synthetic distinction and verificationism,
i.e., the verification theory of meaning as applied to individual
sentences[2]. The first of these empiricist doctrines has, as noted in the
Introduction, its roots in Hume's distinction between relations of ideas
and matters of fact. The second empiricist doctrine that Quine rejects
in "Two Dogmas," verificationism, emerged as the basis of a strategy
of completing one half of Hume's agenda, that of showing how all
empirical knowledge flows from experience.

The publication of "Two Dogmas" is sometimes seen as dating
Quine's break with Carnap and the two core doctrines of the logico-
empiricist tradition. But as Quine himself notes in his Preface to *From
a Logical Point of View* "The critique of analycity to which "Two
Dogmas" is in large part devoted is an outcome of informal
discussions, oral and written, in which I have engaged from 1939
onward with Professors Carnap, Alonzo Church, Nelson Goodman,
Alfred Tarski, and Morton White..." (viii). So at most the publication
dates Quine's public split with Carnap. We have also seen that some of

the roots of the split can also be found in "Truth by Convention," which first appeared in 1936, and in which Quine challenges the view that logic and mathematics are "purely analytic or conventional" (70), that is, without empirical content.

We noted in the Introduction that Quine is concerned with the literary style as well as with the philosophic content of his writings. In "Two Dogmas" he adopts the device of showing that common, and superficially promising, defenses of the analytic/synthetic distinction invariably turn out to presuppose, rather than elucidate, the notion of analyticity. An investigation of the nest of interrelated notions, analyticity, synonymy, interchangeability *salva veritate,* and necessary truth yields, Quine charmingly notes, an argument that "is not flatly circular, but something like it. It has the form, figuratively speaking, of a closed curve in space." (30). We now review the salient pieces of this closed curve in space.

Kant's view, Quine claims, can be taken to be that "a statement is analytic when it is true by virtue of meanings and independently of fact." (21). Quine finds meanings to be "obscure intermediary entities" that are "well abandoned" in favor of an investigation of "the synonymy of linguistic forms." That is, instead of talking of meanings, we can talk, given the notion of synonymy, of two linguistic forms, two sentences or two words, meaning the same if and only if they are synonymous. So we are making progress, if we can give an account of synonymy. The progress is this: analytic statements fall into two sub-classes ("by general philosophical acclaim" (22)): logical truths and statements that can be turned into logical truths "by putting synonyms for synonyms" (23).

Quine's example of a logical truth is "No unmarried man is married" and his general characterization of a logical truth is "a statement which is true and remains true under all reinterpretations of its components other than the logical particles" (22), these exemplified by "'no', 'un-', 'not', 'if', 'then', 'and', *etc.*" An example of a statement that is not a logical truth but yields one through the substitution of synonym for synonym is "No bachelor is married," where 'bachelor' and 'unmarried man' are taken to be synonyms.

This first part of the closed curve seeks to explicate analyticity in terms of synonymy, which, Quine contends, "is no less in need of clarification than analyticity itself" (23). In Section 2 Quine explores and rejects the view that synonymy rests on definition. On this view 'bachelor' is supposedly defined as, and is therefore synonymous with, 'unmarried man' (24). The problem is that ordinary definitions, dictionary definitions, are not stipulations but reports on usage. "The lexicographer is an empirical scientist, whose business is the recording of antecedent facts" (24). That is, the lexicographer reports on linguistic usage, including on the usage of two terms as synonyms for one another. He or she does not create usage or synonyms.

Quine does grant that there is "an extreme sort of definition which does not hark back to prior synonymies at all: namely, the explicitly conventional introduction of novel notations for the purposes of sheer abbreviation" (26). An example is when a logician introduces the expression 'iff' as an abbreviation for 'if and only if'. Thereafter 'iff' means, is synonymous with, is interchangeable with 'if and only if' because the logician has declared that it be so. Although this is, as Quine notes, "a really transparent case of synonymy created by definition," it is clear that such cases of synonymy cannot save the notion of analyticity. Not every analytic truth that is not a logical truth can be turned into a logical truth by appeal to an explicitly conventional introduction of a synonymous term. (See also "Truth by Convention" where Quine argues against the plausibility of the view that mathematics and logic are true by convention).

Quine next turns to the notion of interchangeability of terms *salva veritate* as a possible explication of synonymy. The proposal is that expressions are synonymous if they are everywhere interchangeable *salva veritate,* that is, without changing the truth or falsity of the containing statement. The problem here is that such allegedly clear synonyms as 'bachelor' and 'unmarried male' are not so interchangeable. For example, 'Unmarried male' cannot be substituted for 'Bachelor' in

'Bachelor' has less than ten letters

without turning the above truth into the falsehood

'Unmarried male' has less than ten letters

(Quine's example, 28.) The expression 'unmarried male' contains more, not less, than ten letters. To make the substitutivity test work we have to limit substitutions to whole words. The word spelled b-a-c-h-e-l-o-r does not occur as a whole word in the above example, though its name, which is formed by placing single quotation marks around that word, does. Appearances notwithstanding, the word we are discussing that is allegedly synonymous with the expression 'unmarried male' no more appears in

'Bachelor' has less than ten letters

than does the word 'cat' in 'catapult'.

So far so good (assuming the notion of 'wordhood' is unproblematic). But to make the substitutivity test work–to prevent its declaring such co-referential but non-synonymous expressions as 'the first President of the United States' [under the Constitution] and 'the second husband of Martha Washington' synonymous–we will have to consider substitutivity not only within such ordinary contexts as

The first President of the United States was married to Martha Washington

but also such contexts as

Necessarily the first President of the United States was married to Martha Washington.

That is, while the expressions 'the first President of the United States' and 'the second husband of Martha Washington' are intersubstitutable in the first context, *salva veritate*, they are not in the second.

Necessarily the first President of the United States was married to Martha Washington

is presumably false while

Necessarily the second husband of Martha Washington was married to Martha Washington

is presumably true.

But, Quine now reminds us, to attach 'necessarily' to a statement is just to claim that the statement is analytic. That is,

Necessarily bachelors are unmarried

is best understood as

'Bachelors are unmarried' is analytic.

So our curve in space has closed itself. We can explicate analyticity in terms of synonymy, synonymy in terms of intersubstitutivity *salve veritate*, including in contexts governed by 'necessarily', and such necessity in terms of analyticity.[3]

Quine next turns his attention to his second target, "The Verification Theory and Reductionism." Historically, discussions of "Two Dogmas of Empiricism" have centered on Quine's attack on the analytic/synthetic distinction and have largely ignored the second dogma, verificationism (perhaps because many defenders of the analytic/synthetic distinction, for example Strawson, Grice, and

25

Alston, have no sympathy for verificationism). And indeed at first it seems odd that Quine would see these two positions as paired or related dogmas. Upon reflection one might conclude that having rejected the analytic/synthetic distinction, Quine had no choice but to also reject verificationism, precisely because he does not want to abandon the meaningfulness of logic and mathematics. That is, if the only criterion of meaningfulness is verification by sensory experience, then mathematics and logic appear to be meaningless; for surely there are no sensory experiences that can be taken to confirm (or disconfirm) the alleged truths of mathematics and logic. This unlikely view of logic and mathematics as consisting of important nonsense is in fact one A.J. Ayer was willing to take in his explication and defense of verificationism in *Language, Truth, and Logic.* Being unwilling to follow Ayer in proclaiming mathematics and logic to be "important nonsense," one might conclude that Quine has no choice but to reject verificationism as a theory of meaning.

But this is not the motivation for Quine's rejection of verificationism. Quine does not take the truths of mathematics and logic to be unverified by the standards of verificationism. Quine writes

> ...as long as it is taken to be significant in general to speak of the confirmation and infirmation of a statement, it seems significant to speak also of a limiting kind of statement which is vacuously confirmed, *ipso facto,* come what may; and such a statement is analytic (41).

That is, Quine grants that "the truth of statements does obviously depend both upon language and upon extralinguistic fact" (41). If we allow sentences to be candidates for truth and falsity individually, taken one-by-one, it follows that we can explicate analytic sentences as the limiting case, those in which "the linguistic component is all that matters...," where the role of extralinguistic fact is nil. Given verificationism, the truths of logic and mathematics and perhaps all commonly termed analytic statements are vacuously verified, verified "come what may" by way of experience.

Hence, were verificationism to stand it would, by itself, constitute a basis for an explication (and thus reinstitution) of the analytic/synthetic distinction, analytic statements being those that are verified come what may. So if the analytic/synthetic distinction is to be banished as an unsupportable dogma, so must verificationism. In fact, Quine asserts not just that the analytic/synthetic distinction is a consequence of verificationism, but also that "The two dogmas are, indeed, at root identical" (41).

It is not, in fact, immediately obvious that verificationism does follows from the analytic/synthetic distinction, that is, that the two are identical. We return to this issue below. We turn now to Quine's attack on verificationism.

It is worth noting that Quine holds verificationism to be very closely connected with, if not equivalent to, radical reductionism–the view that "Every meaningful statement is... translatable into a statement (true or false) about immediate experience" (38). Quine's argument against verificationism, and radical reductionism, takes the form of what might be called "dismissal by charitable reinterpretation." Radical reductionism goes back at least to Locke and Hume, who "held that every idea must either originate directly in sense experience or else be compounded of ideas thus originating" (38). Tooke improved on this idea by moving the focus from ideas to terms, allowing the doctrine to be rephrased in "semantical terms by saying that a term, to be significant at all, must be either a name of a sense datum or a compound of such names or an abbreviation of such a compound" (38). But such a doctrine, Quine maintains, is

> unnecessarily and intolerably restrictive in the term-by-term critique which it imposes. More reasonably, and without yet exceeding the limits of what I have called radical reductionism, we may take full statements as our significant units–thus demanding that our statements as wholes be translatable into sense-datum language, but not that they be translatable term by term" (38-39).

Devising such a translation scheme for statements into sense-datum language was the goal of Carnap's *Aufbau*. Although Quine finds Carnap's attempt, and especially his constructions utilizing "the whole language of pure mathematics" (39) impressive, he believes the whole project is ultimately doomed to failure, because Carnap

> provides no indication, not even the sketchiest, of how a statement of the form 'Quality q is at $x;y;z;t$' [a point instant] could ever be translated into Carnap's initial language of sense data and logic. The connective 'is at' remains an added undefined connective; the canons counsel us in its use but not in its elimination (40).

Carnap abandoned his radical reductionism project subsequently to publishing the *Aufbau*. Others continued to hold that

> ...to each statement, or each synthetic statement, there is associated a unique range of possible sensory events such that the occurrence of any of them would add to the likelihood of truth of the statement, and that there is associated also another unique range of possible sensory events whose occurrence would detract from that likelihood (40-41).

Quine does not now produce and criticize the arguments of those who continued to hold the above view after Carnap abandoned it. Rather, Quine makes a "counter suggestion"–a charitable reinterpretation of the verificationism and radical reductionism of the *Aufbau*–namely that "our statements about the external world face the tribunal of sense experience not individually but only as a corporate body" (41).

The counter suggestion is, of course, holism–one of the two key doctrines that Quine was to spend the rest of his career elucidating and defending (the other being the explication of how experience does constrain theories, that is, of how we can have holism and empiricism).

The arguments Quine gives against the analytic/synthetic distinction, the "closed curve in space" we explored above, are not decisive arguments. Quine's strategy is rather to put the onus on those who want to rehabilitate the analytic/synthetic distinction. And this he does. His challenge is, in effect, this: If the analytic/synthetic distinction is to be maintained, then either the notion of meaning must be resuscitated and clearly enough explicated so as to provide grounds for deciding whether the "meaning" of one term is or is not included within that of another term (Kant's original notion); or the notion of cognitive synonymy must be explicated, without appealing to analyticity; or the notion of substitutivity *salva veritate* must be explicated, without appealing to contexts that presuppose analyticity but are strong enough to distinguish between co-extensionality and synonymy. Since the publication of "Two Dogmas" Quine's critics have taken up this challenge, offering views of meaning or synonymy, or of modal operators such as 'necessarily', that purport to break the "closed curve in space." None, in the opinion of the present authors, succeeds.

As noted earlier, it is interesting, as a comment about Quine and his intellectual indebtedness, that Quine argues directly and in some detail against Carnap. In almost no other work does Quine take on the views of another philosopher in this kind of detail, with this directness. He generally attacks commonly held positions with broad strokes, not positions unique to a single philosopher, and not in this detail (except in his invited responses to various essays about his own work). We think this is a testament to how indebted Quine feels to Carnap.

Quine's rejection of verificationism sparked far less discussion than did his rejection of the analytic/synthetic distinction, perhaps because verificationism was already becoming shopworn and out-of-fashion by the time "Two Dogmas" appeared, or at least by the time it became well-known. Those who reject Quine's holism do not generally do so in favor of some form of verificationism. Rather, they generally argue for, or presuppose, some version of a correspondence theory of truth, and a realism that grants to middle sized physical objects, or molecules, or atoms and sub-atomic particles, or whatever, some status other than posits of our best going theories. That is, Quine's discussion of verificationism occurs, as it were, within the family of empiricist views that grant a special status to experience or some refinement of it (firings of sensory receptors); within that family, but not within the wider philosophical community, verificationism and holism exhaust the available options.

Finally, we return to Quine's claim (generally neglected in the literature) that the "two dogmas are... at root identical." If they are, then those who find verificationism implausible or unacceptable should take the same view towards the purported distinction between analytic and synthetic statements. Quine's argument to the effect that if verificationism can be defended then so too can the analytic/synthetic distinction, is reasonably clear and has already been reviewed. Is there an implicit argument in the other direction? Perhaps. If there is an analytic/synthetic distinction, then it makes sense to distinguish the role of linguistic convention and the role of extralinguistic fact in determining the truth or falsity of a given statement. Analytic statements are those where "the linguistic component is all that matters." Synthetic statements are those whose truth-values are not determined by the linguistic component alone. So if we are able to distinguish analytic statements from synthetic ones, it must be that we are able to identify the factors that determine their truth-values, the linguistic and non-linguistic components, on a statement by statement basis. So for each synthetic statement we can identify the extralinguistic elements, the elements of experience, that are relevant to its truth or falsity. But then we are free to identify the meaning of the statement with those extra-linguistic elements. And this is just what verificationism does. So, in this sense, verificationism does follow from the analytic/synthetic distinction, if one is prepared to identify meaning with the experiences relevant to a synthetic statement's truth or falsity. Traditional empiricists were ready to do this, but not all contemporary philosophers are traditional empiricists.

The rejection of the analytic/synthetic distinction and verificationism opens the door to holism. Holism is a substantial and consequential doctrine, and is central to Quine's defense of empiricism without dogmas.

The classic statement of Quinean holism is in fact given in "Empiricism without the Dogmas," the last section of "Two Dogmas." It is worth quoting at length:

> The totality of our so-called knowledge or beliefs, from the most casual matters of geography and history to the profoundest laws of atomic physics or even of pure mathematics and logic, is a man-made fabric which impinges on experience only along the edges. Or, to change the figure, total science is like a field of force whose boundary conditions are experience. A conflict with experience at the periphery occasions readjustments in the interior of the field. Truth values have to be redistributed over some of our statements. Reëvaluation of some statements entails reëvaluation of others, because of their logical interconnections–the logical laws being in turn simply certain further statements of the system, certain further elements of the field... But the total field is so underdetermined by its boundary conditions, experience, that there is much latitude of choice as to what statements to reëvaluate in the light of any single contrary experience. No particular experiences are linked with any particular statements in the interior of the field, except indirectly through considerations of equilibrium affecting the field as a whole (42-43).

In "Two Dogmas" holism is offered as a counter-suggestion to the two dogmas Quine views as "at root identical." But there is, in "Two Dogmas," no full blown argument for holism, no lengthy explication of it, and no exploration of how it transforms empiricism.

We will have much more to say about holism in the next chapter. Here it is worth noting that while the above is the classic statement of Quine's holism, there are precursors to it in Quine's earlier writings. In "Truth by Convention," first published in 1936, Quine argues that conventional definitions do not really establish a separate kind of truth–'truth by convention'. Quine says there of "the apparent contrast between logico-mathematical truths and others"

> Viewed behavioristically and without reference to a metaphyhsical system, this contrast retains reality as a contrast between more and less firmly accepted statements... There are statements which we choose to surrender last, if at all, in the course of revamping our sciences in the face of new discoveries; and among these there are some we will not surrender at all, so basic are they to our whole conceptual scheme. Among the latter are to be counted the so-called truths of logic and mathematics, regardless of what further we may have to say of their status in the course of a subsequent sophisticated philosophy (95).

Endnotes

[1] Two Dogmas of Empiricism," 30.

[2] Quine's target in "Two Dogmas" is verificationism as promulgated by the members of the Vienna Circle. That is, he is attacking the view that individual sentences have empirical content and that that content is "the method of empirically confirming or infirming" them. Quine's own view, as we will see in this and later chapters, is that most individual sentences have meaning only to the extent that they are parts of larger theories or chunks of theories that can be tested against experience. That is, verificationism works as a theory of meaning of larger linguistic units–whole theories or significant chunks thereof. As we will see in Chapter 5, verificationism also does work for a special class of sentences (observation sentences and their kin).

[3] We have omitted portions of Quine's arguments directed specifically at Carnap's defenses of the analytic/synthetic distinction. They are of some historical interest but are not central to Quine's basic argument.

4

Holism

Wie Schiffer sind wir, die ihr Schiff auf offener See umbauen müssen,
ohne es jemals in einem Dock zerlegen und aus besten Bestandteilen
neu errichten zu können.

– Otto Neurath[1]

The Doctrine and Its Sources

In "Two Dogmas of Empiricism," Quine offers holism as an
alternative to verificationism, and as an account of how sentences
previously taken to be analytic (the claims of logic and mathematics)
can be counted as meaningful. Holism is a substantial and significant
doctrine; it argues for the tentativeness of all of our theories and beliefs,
from the most theoretical of the theoretical sciences to the most down
to earth common-sense theories and beliefs. If it is correct,
correspondence theories of truth go by the board and, with them, any
possibility of construing empiricism is a theory of truth. Holism argues
against the plausibility of "meta-level" theories of truth and *for* truth as
immanent, *a la* Tarski. If there is a future for empiricism it is as a
theory of evidence: a theory about how the evidence provided by our
sensory receptors serves as the basis for warranted beliefs, and of how
language does contribute to "meaning" but not in a way that can be
isolated on a sentence by sentence basis.

If holism holds, foundationalism also goes by the board; there are
no Archimedean standpoints. We work, to paraphrase Quine, as
scientists, lay persons, and philosophers, *from within*–from the vantage
point of an evolving body of theory we inherit and seek to improve, on
the basis of experiences significantly shaped by this very same body of

theory. Working from within this theory, we indeed take the claims we find to be warranted to be true. But truth is immanent and the firmest of warrants is provisional (1981a, 22).

Quine often uses Neurath's metaphor, quoted above, that likens us (scientists, philosophers, and everyone else) to sailors who must rebuild their ship, plank by plank, while staying afloat in it. Here is a similar characterization from "On Mental Entities":

> As scientists we accept provisionally our heritage from the dim past, with intermediate revisions by our more recent forebears; and then we continue to warp and revise (210).

As we have already noted, fleshing out holism's implications for empiricism (and for science broadly construed to include common-sense theorizing and epistemology) is a project to which Quine has returned again and again since the publication of "Two Dogmas."

We begin our explication of holism by identifying two theses that are intertwined with it. In Chapter 3, we quoted the classic statement of holism given in the last section of "Two Dogmas." The passage begins:

> The totality of our so-called knowledge or beliefs, from the most casual matters of geography and history to the profoundest laws of atomic physics or even of pure mathematics and logic, is a man-made fabric which impinges on experience only along the edges.

The first intertwined thesis is thus that all of science broadly construed is our own construction, and that even the apparently most disparate parts are, in fact, interconnected–hence Quine's metaphor of a fabric (and of a network, a field, and a web).

The same paragraph of "Two Dogmas" contains this passage:

> A conflict with experience at the periphery occasions readjustments in the interior of the field. Truth values have to be redistributed over some of our statements. Reëvaluation of some statements entails reëvaluation of others, because of their logical interconnections–the logical laws being in turn simply certain further statements of the system, certain further elements of the field... But the total field is so underdetermined by its boundary conditions, experience, that there is much latitude of choice as to what statements to reëvaluate in the light of any single contrary experience.

This is the second intertwined thesis, that a recalcitrant experience can force an adjustment in the network of theories to which we are committed, to the totality of science. But such an experience cannot force a change of commitment to any particular belief or component sentence of science. This is because

> No particular experiences are linked with any particular statements in the interior of the field, except indirectly through considerations of equilibrium affecting the field as a whole.

And this is the overarching thesis of holism: that our theories of nature face experience as a collective body, not sentence by sentence, not even particular theory by particular theory. They do so because there is no one-to-one relationship between most sentences of this body and specific experiences. The thesis of holism, we can now see, is a consequence of taking the verification theory of meaning seriously, the thesis that a chunk of language has empirical meaning only if there are experiences that will confirm or disconfirm it. There are no such confirming or disconfirming experiences for most individual sentences. There are for sentences taken collectively, for bodies of theory, for our whole going theory of the world (for science broadly construed). So it is only sentences taken collectively–bodies of theory, or our whole going theory of the world–that have or has empirical meaning. Empirical meaning or content is spread across the sentences that together can be tested against experience.

And thus it is that, faced with recalcitrant experience or inter-theoretic conflicts, we make decisions concerning which sentence or sentences of a theory to regard as vulnerable, and which to hold firm. Theoretical virtues, such as conservatism, simplicity, fecundity, and so forth, figure in such decisions; but neither they nor experiments dictate a particular outcome. All of our theories, and all of our judgments concerning them, are tentative. How large or how all-embracing a network of sentences must be to have empirical content, is not yet clear. (Some individual sentences do meet the verificationist test for empirical meaningfulness–observation sentences and their kin. We will explore this restricted group of sentences in Chapter 5.)

It is obvious, at least upon reflection, that the empirical content of the more obviously esoteric sentences which figure in scientific theories and practice is a function of the broader body of theory in which those sentences are contained. Consider, for example,

> These chipped stones, found near fossil remains of *Australopithecus*, indicate tool use.

> Members of species tend to behave in ways that maximize their fitness.

> The vibrations of this spot of light on this celluloid ruler measure the electrical resistance of that coil (Duhem 1991, 145).

The first and third are singular sentences, sentences about particular objects and events. The second is a generalization; it says of each and every thing that is a member of a species that it will behave in certain ways. Each presupposes extensive and sophisticated bodies of theory. The first presupposes notions of fossils, a now extinct species, and tools. It further presupposes a body of theory that makes it plausible to link chipped stones with tool making. The second sentence is from evolutionary theory, and the notion of "fitness" it presupposes is technical and varies by school of thought. Sociobiologists, for example, define an organism's "fitness" in terms of the number of its genes that get replicated in the next generation. The notion of "species" is also theoretical, and has evolved a pace with developments in science (for example, in genetics). The third sentence is a singular sentence, but the general theory about electricity it presupposes allows for the sentence to be appropriately uttered within the context of any number of similar experiments. And it is a substantial body of theory that relates the spot of light to the electrical resistance of the coil. As Pierre Duhem noted, if a novice asked the researcher undertaking this experiment what the relationship is between the electrical resistance of a coil and the phenomena perceived, the researcher will recommend that the novice take a course in electricity (Duhem 1991, 145).

Substantial bodies of theory are also presupposed in scientific predictions. Consider:

> Tools used in conjunction with hunting or gathering will be found near fossil remains of *Australopithecus*.

> Female lions will display behaviors that will tend to increase the number of their genes replicated in the next generation.

> If an observer "plunges the metallic stem of a rod, mounted with rubber into small holes, the iron [will oscillate] and, by means of a mirror tied to it, [send] a beam of light over to a celluloid ruler" (Duhem 1991, 145).

Behind each prediction lies a substantial body of theory. Should one of these predictions not be borne out (should we be able to find no tools near the fossil remains of early hominids, should female lions consistently behave in ways that work against their reproductive success, should no beams of light be sent to a celluloid ruler in later experiments), we will need to make adjustments somewhere in the

35

theory that yielded the prediction. But the failed prediction does not itself identify where the adjustments should be made. Indeed, the problem might not lie in the specific body of theory with which we associate the prediction. As his references to "the totality of our so-called knowledge and beliefs" indicate, Quine holds that empirical content is shared more broadly than our assumptions about boundaries separating the sciences from one another, or from common sense, would suggest. Recall this passage from *Word and Object*.

> Theory may be deliberate, as in a chapter on chemistry, or it may be second nature, as is the immemorial doctrine of ordinary enduring middle-sized objects. In either case, theory causes a sharing, by sentences, of sensory supports. In an arch, the overhead block is supported immediately by other overhead blocks, and ultimately by all the base blocks collectively and none individually; and so it is with sentences, when theoretically fitted (11).

In other words, the sentences of the various sciences, and those of common sense, are in some significant way interdependent.

We can get a sense of the interdependence reflected in Quine's use of an arch metaphor by remembering the structure he attributes to the network of theories we maintain. There are sentences "deeply embedded" in the network (in the "interior" both in the sense that they are furthest from the periphery of experience, and interwoven through other theories); sentences "closest to the periphery" of experience; and a host of sentences in between. The characterization of holism that appears in "Two Dogmas," and that just cited from *Word and Object*, suggest the view that the more embedded a sentence is, the more its relationship to specific stimulus conditions is a function of (is mediated by) other sentences.

Quine's discussion in "Posits and Reality" of what he there called "the molecular doctrine" pulls together the foregoing points. When the essay was written, the technologies that now enable molecules to be observed had not been developed. In this sense, but only in this sense, Quine's discussion is dated. What he says about the evidence supporting theories that posit molecules applies to all theories, including our common-sense physical-object theory.

> According to physics, my desk is, for all its seeming fixity and solidity, a swarm of vibrating molecules... no glimpse is to be had of the separate molecules of the desk; they are, we are told, too small.

Lacking such experience, what evidence can the physicist muster for his doctrine of molecules? His answer is that there is a convergence of indirect evidence, drawn from such varied phenomena as expansion, heat conduction, capillary attraction, and surface tension. The point is that these miscellaneous phenomena can, if we assume the molecular theory, be marshaled under the familiar laws of motion... [A]ny defense of [the molecular doctrine] has to do... with its indirect bearing on observable reality. The doctrine has this indirect bearing by being the core of an integrated physical theory which implies truths about expansion, conduction, and so on (233-35).

On the one hand, theories that posit molecules (or other physical particles too small to directly observe) provide systematic explanations of a wide range of phenomena, including common-sense phenomena. This, together with other virtues of the doctrine of molecules (such as simplicity, familiarity of principle, and scope), are among the benefits of adopting the theory. On the other hand, what warrants such theories, *i.e.*, what constitutes evidence for them, is their ability to link sensory stimulations to sensory stimulations. This criterion applies to all theories.

Having noticed that man has no evidence for the existence of bodies beyond the fact that their assumption helps him to organize experience, we should [do] well, instead of disclaiming evidence for the existence of bodies, to conclude: such, then, at bottom, is what evidence is, both for ordinary bodies and for molecules (238).

It may seem that while clearly theoretical sentences have empirical meaning only within the broader context of their containing theories, as holism asserts, this is not so for more mundane sentences, such as 'The mail carrier will come again tomorrow' or 'There is an apple on the counter'. But there is also a substantial body of theory lying behind even these claims. As we explore in some detail in Chapter 5, Quine maintains that common-sense sentences about bodies (about mail carriers and apples) presuppose physical object theory, a theory which maintains that there are middle-sized objects (such that we say "here's an apple," rather than "it's apple-ing"), of which apples are examples (but "red" and "on" are not). To learn physical object theory is to learn that apples and lots of other things are discrete objects (unlike snow which is scattered about in blankets or drifts), and we learn this theory as we learn language and master the principles of

37

individuation (as we learn 'a', 'the', 'an', and so forth). Such principles, together with the notion (also part of physical object theory) that middle-sized objects are relatively enduring, makes it possible to wonder, to paraphrase Quine, if the apple on the counter is the one noticed yesterday.

We have only begun to scratch the surface in terms of what this relatively simple sentence presupposes (consider, for example, the "is" of predication, and the predicate 'is on the counter'). But perhaps it is sufficient to understand what Quine is urging. Even if we learn this particular sentence by mimicry (by adults pointing repeatedly to the relevant scene and repeating the sentence until we come to repeat it in appropriately similar situations), we don't learn every sentence this way. The child who masters this sentence will eventually be able to come up with 'My doll is on the table', and 'My doll is *not* on the table', never having heard either sentence. At this point, we say that she or he "has caught on" to at least some of our most basic *theory* of the world concomitantly with catching on to our theory of language.

This same body of theory, which tells us what to expect by way of the behavior of various kinds of objects, can yield the prediction "If no one has eaten it, this apple will still be on the counter in the morning." "Seeing a body *again*," Quine notes, "means to us that it or we or our glance has returned from a round trip in the course of which the body was out of sight" (1987a, 204; emphasis added). The notion of 'seeing again' requires a sophisticated notion of "the corporeality of things" (1087a, 204). In *Quiddities*, Quine explores the way in which the empirical content of common-sense sentences about ordinary bodies depends on physical object theory.

> William James pictured the baby's senses as first assailed by a "blooming, buzzing confusion." In the fullness of time a sorting out sets in. "Hello," he has the infant wordlessly noting, "Thingumbob again!"
>
> Thingumbob: a rattle, perhaps, or a bottle, a ball, a towel, a mother? Or it may only have been sunshine, a cool breeze, a snatch of maternal babytalk: they are all on an equal footing on first acquaintance. Later we come to recognize corporeal things as the substantial foundation of nature. The very word 'thing' connotes bodies first and foremost, and it takes some effort to appreciate that the corporeal sense of 'thing' is peculiarly sophisticated (1987a, 204).

"The corporeal sense of 'thing'" presupposes what Quine in *Word and Object* calls "the immemorial doctrine of ordinary enduring middle-sized objects" (11). We consider the positions just outlined in more detail in Chapters 5 and 7. Here we note that it is an implication of the several arguments we have summarized that most sentences, of common sense as well as of science, have empirical content only as part of broader bodies of theory–and that it is such broader bodies that yield predictions.

How extensive a portion of our currently maintained theories need we consider in making a judgment about any particular hypothesis or claim? Much more, of course, than just the hypothesis or claim in question. But normally, Quine maintains, we do not need to consider the whole of a going theory of nature to adjudicate some specific hypothesis or theory. Rather, he suggests that what he terms a "moderate or relative holism" will generally suffice (1960, 13). "What is important," Quine suggests in "Five Milestones of Empiricism," "is that we cease to demand or expect of a scientific sentence that it have its own separable empirical meaning" (71). There is more to explore concerning the scope of holism, and we return to it in the next chapter.

The Implications of Holism

We noted at the outset that holism argues for the tentativeness of all of our theories and theorizing. Lacking an algorithm or formula for determining what sentence or sentences some set of observations confirms or falsifies, there is no place for dogmatism. As lay persons and scientists we enjoy far less certainty, and must make far more choices, than suggested by simpler theories of the relationship between science and sensory experience. A further implication of holism is that we have no "unmediated access" to the world around us. We work within a network of theories we inherit, and do our part to contribute to them. And this network itself is connected multifariously to experience, directly confronting it only at the edges.

We also noted that, if holism is correct, correspondence theories of truth go by the board because we are not in a position to relate most sentences, taken individually, to stimulus conditions that would verify them, and because correspondence theories presuppose a dichotomy between theories and the world, or language and the world. The only relationship reasonably explored is that between systems of sentences and the triggerings of our sensory receptors, a relationship that more appropriately underwrites the notion of warranted belief than it does the notion of truth. Empiricism emerges as a theory of evidence.

Endnotes

[1] As quoted by Quine 1960, vii.

5
Empiricism Reconstituted

The relation to be analyzed, then, is the relation between our sensory stimulations and our scientific theory formulations: the relation between the physicist's sentences on the one hand, treating of gravitation and electrons and the like, and on the other hand the triggering of his sensory receptors.

– W.V. Quine[1]

We cannot rest with a running conceptualization of the unsullied stream of experience; what we need is a sullying of the stream.

– W.V. Quine[2]

By the end of "Two Dogmas" we are left without two fundamental theses of empiricism, the analytic/synthetic distinction and verificationism (theses that Quine takes to be, at bottom, the same thesis). Empiricism itself may seem to be in shambles, for while we have a sketch of holism, it is only a sketch: we are told that "...our statements about the external world face the tribunal of sense experience not individually but only as a corporate body" (1963b, 41), but not a great deal more. As importantly, as Quine himself noted years later, "My noncommittal term 'experience' awaited a theory" (1981c, 40).

In Chapter 4, we explored Quine's arguments for holism. We noted two of its more significant implications: that recalcitrant experiences or inter–theoretic conflicts do not themselves dictate which sentences of theories to hold vulnerable and which to hold firm, and that correspondence theories of truth go by the board. If Quine is to escape the charge of relativism, if he is to preserve the empirical core of the logico–empiricist tradition, he has to find some characterization of experience on which experience so construed makes some theories better bets than other theories. He has to have an account of how language, which is avowedly part of the world, "hooks up with" the non-linguistic part of the world. He has to come up with an account of empirical content that derives from some reconstituted notion of experience and spreads itself across our theories generally, including the most abstract parts of mathematics and logic.

Whatever this reconstituted notion of experience is, it will not be a phenomenological notion. Quine rejects ideas as the meanings of words (*i.e.*, he rejects non-linguistic word meaning as a viable notion). His objection to ideas is not that they cannot, in principle, be explicated, but rather that they have not been explicated–we lack identity conditions for them–and that they serve no useful purpose. Words will do as well, and sentences will do better than words, and theories better than sentences, as the bearers of meaning (empirical content). As we noted in Chapter 2, it is not much of a caricature of his view to say that if we needed ideas, as the building blocks of meaning, and thence of sentences and theories, Quine would work hard to reconstitute them. But we don't, and he doesn't.

But in another sense Quine does need something like ideas. Traditional empiricists, from Locke to Carnap, thought that there is some specifiable content of experience that constitutes the foundation of all science. This content took the form of ideas for Locke and Berkeley, impressions and ideas for Hume, sense data for Carnap and some logical positivists. Quine does not need ideas, or even a cleaned up version of ideas, as the meanings of words, because he doesn't need (non-linguistic) word meaning. But he does care about empirical content, and he needs some source and loci of such content. So he does have to work to reconstruct, if not ideas, then sense experience. And it is hard work. For the traditional theory of sense-experience or sense data as immediately given and directly apparent is nearly as problematic as is the notion that the meanings of words are ideas.

> We may hold, with Berkeley, that the momentary data of vision consist of colors disposed in a spatial manifold of two dimensions; but we come to this conclusion by reasoning from the bidimensionality of the ocular surface, or by noting the illusions which can be engendered by two-dimensional artifacts such as paintings and mirrors... Again we may hold that the momentary data of audition are clusters of components each of which is a function of just two variables, pitch and loudness; but not without knowledge of the physical variables of frequency and amplitude in the stimulating string... (1960, 2).

Moreover

> ...immediate experience simply will not, of itself, cohere as an autonomous domain. References to physical things are largely

41

what hold it together. These references are not just inessential vestiges of the initially intersubjective character of language, capable of being weeded out by devising an artificially subjective language for sense data. Rather they give us our main continuing access to past sense data themselves; for past sense data are mostly gone for good except as commemorated in physical posits (1960, 2-3).

So the reconstructed notion of experience Quine is after will be arrived at by making full use of the findings of science. It will be conceptually dependent upon, not conceptually prior to, our notions of enduring objects and macro events. It will rest on the findings of anatomy and physiology as well as optics and acoustics and much else. There is no reason to think, in fact there is every reason to deny, that we are directly aware of the sense experiences that will provide the empirical content Quine is after. Nor will such experiences yield certainty; but they must be able to give content, however indirectly, to all of our knowledge claims.

In "Two Dogmas" Quine talks of "sensory events" and of "sense experience" as replacements for Carnap's sense data. In the opening pages of *Word and Object* he talks of the "impacts at our nerve endings" and of "activated retinas" (2), and later of "stimulatory occasions" (9), "surface irritations" (26), and "stimulations" (30), and of "the triggerings of sensory receptors." In "Things and Their Place in Theories" he talks of episodes of "sensory stimulation" (1) and, again, of the "triggering of our sensory receptors" (1). And in *Pursuit of Truth*, Quine talks of "sensory stimulation."

> By the stimulation undergone by a subject on a given occasion I just mean the temporally ordered set of all those of his exteroceptors that are triggered on that occasion (2).

The notion of sensory events as being the source of all empirical content, with those events construed as the firings of sensory receptors—each episode of which, neuroscience tells us, is to be construed as "the temporally ordered set of all those of... [the subject's] exteroceptors that are triggered on that occasion"–seems clear enough. It gives content enough to the blank check Quine issued in "Two Dogmas" when he talked just of "experience." At least we will here presume it does. But how do such non-linguistic events as the triggerings of exteroceptors connect up with language and provide empirical content for all of science, for common sense theorizing, and for the theorizing of philosophers?

Quine's answer is through a stimulus-response analysis of subjects' verbal behavior in stimulatory situations with regard to selected sentences construed holophrastically. This takes some considerable explanation.

Quine uses two vehicles to develop and explain his theory of the relation between language and experience, and of how experience constitutes the evidence for all our theories: the way children learn language and the way a field linguist develops a translation manual for a language that is wholly unknown to the linguist. (Quine calls the latter "radical translation.") In both cases the notion of a one-word sentence–either a sentence that is literally a single word, or a multi-word sentence that is "construed holophrastically" as if it were one long word–is pivotal.

> Any realistic theory of evidence must be inseparable from the psychology of stimulus and response, applied to sentences (1960, 17).

Quine's theory of evidence is, at bottom, an account of how experience construed as the firings of sensory receptors, generates assent to or dissent from sentences construed holophrastically, and how from those sentences empirical content spreads out across our full theory of the world.

In *Word and Object* Quine introduces his exploration of the relation between language and experience thus:

> 'Ouch' is a one-word sentence which a man may volunteer from time to time by way of laconic comment on the passing show (5).

'Ouch', though a single word, constitutes a full sentence, one that cannot be used as a constituent of longer sentence in the way that most words can, *e.g.*, 'red', 'water', and 'mama'. But words such as the latter can be used, like 'ouch', as one-word sentences. Indeed, Quine suggests that infants normally do learn such expressions as 'red', 'water', and 'mama' as one-word sentences. When well learned, each is uttered "in the appropriate presences, or as means of inducing the appropriate presences" (1969a, 7). As we saw in Chapter 4, Quine maintains that, at this level, one-word sentences serve as feature noting or summoning devices, with no referential import: "...the mother, red, and water are for the infant all of a type: each is just a history of sporadic encounter, a scattered portion of what goes on" (1969a, 7). There is no individuation of objects here.

In Quine's story of the field linguist doing radical translation, the problem at hand is how to construe the expression 'Gavagai', which the

43

linguist has observed members of the population she is studying (let us call them the Antorians) utter on various occasions. The expression is, Quine argues, initially best construed as a one-word sentence, with both the question of constituent words (*e.g.*, is 'Gavagai' really 'Ga vag ai') and of reference (individuation) being deferred. That is, in the initial stages, the linguist's use of 'Gavagai' is analogous to the infant's use of 'mama'–no act of individuation is involved. By querying "Gavagai?" in a variety of situations she can discover when the Antorians will assent to that question and when they will dissent from it, and we are supposing that she discovers that they in fact generally assent when one or more rabbit (or rabbit look-alikes) is in observable proximity, and not otherwise. (1960, 26-30.)

But this by itself does not allow the linguist to conclude that 'gavagai' is a general term of the Antorian language and that the Antorians include rabbits as elements of the domain of their theory of the world. At this stage, equally good translations of 'Gavagai' are 'It rabbiteth', 'Lo, a rabbit', and 'Rabbithood manifest', all construed holophrastically, as one word sentences. And construed holophrastically, these sentences carry commitments neither to rabbiting events, nor to rabbits, nor to the universal rabbithood.

In expanding his account of language learning (whether by a field linguist or by an infant) and his theory of evidence (and the two go hand-in-hand), Quine distinguishes between occasion sentences and standing sentences:

> *Occasion* sentences, as against *standing* sentences, are sentences such as 'Gavagai', 'Red', 'It Hurts', 'His face is dirty', which command assent or dissent only if queried after an appropriate prompting stimulation (1960, 35-36).

Examples of standing sentences, on the other hand, are 'The crocuses are out' and 'The *Times* has come.'

> ...these standing sentences contrast with occasion sentences in that the subject may repeat his old assent or dissent unprompted by current stimulation when we ask him again on later occasions, whereas an occasion sentence commands assent or dissent only as prompted all over again by current stimulation (1960, 36).

The idea is that current stimulation is all, or nearly all, to occasion sentences, and is nothing, or nearly nothing, to standing sentences. That is, whether an Antorian will assent to or dissent from 'Gavagai?' depends nearly entirely on what stimulations the informant is experiencing at or just before the query is made. But the well informed among us will assent to 'Amelia Earhart was the first woman to cross the Atlantic by plane' no matter what our current stimulatory situation may be (barring, *e.g.*, unconsciousness). Quine grants that "Standing sentences grade off toward occasion sentences..." (1960, 36) and worries a good bit about what constitutes an occasion (how long), but this is a finer point we can here pass over. He defines

> The affirmative stimulus meaning of a sentence such as 'Gavagai', for a given speaker, as the class of all stimulations (hence evolving ocular irradiation patterns between properly timed blindfoldings) that would prompt his assent... We may define the *negative* stimulus meaning similarly with 'assent' and 'dissent' interchanged, and then define the *stimulus meaning* as the ordered pair of the two (1960, 32-33).

We now have, Quine believes, "the makings of a crude concept of empirical meaning. For meaning, supposedly, is what a sentence shares with its translation" (1960, 32). And in the envisioned case we have empirical evidence (a history of assents to, and dissents from, "Gavagai?") that the stimulus meaning of 'Rabbit', construed as a one word sentence, is for the linguist identical, near enough, to the stimulus meaning of 'Gavagai' for the Antorians. 'Rabbit' and 'Gavagai' mean the same thing; *i.e.*, they have the same stimulus meaning.[3]

Occasion sentences are, at least in the first instance (that is, in the language learning instance), either one-word sentences, or multiple word sentences construed holophrastically. The constituent words of the latter are to be seen as parts of the sentence only in the uninteresting way that 'ant' is part of 'cantankerous'. This is so because the stimulus-response based procedure used to establish their stimulus meanings works only on whole occasion sentences. (We presume that most standing sentences are not one-word sentences.)

We said above that current stimulation is all, or nearly all, to occasion sentences. This requires refinement. Quine takes observation sentences to be a subset of occasion sentences, and for them, observation sentences, current stimulation *is* all, or nearly all. The difference between occasion sentences that are not observation sentences and those that are lies in the relevance of collateral information. Quine's example is 'Bachelor'. This is an occasion sentence, for we can fix its stimulus meaning for an individual by querying 'Bachelor?' under a variety of situations and identifying those that yield an affirmative response and those that yield a negative response. But the responses are determined not just by present stimulations but also by the queried party's knowledge of social relations. "For any two speakers whose social contacts are not virtually identical, the stimulus meanings of 'Bachelor' will diverge" (1960, 42). So for most pairs of individuals, 'Bachelor' will not have the same stimulus meaning, and thus will not count as an observation sentence.

> Occasion sentences whose stimulus meanings vary none under the influence of collateral information may naturally be called *observation sentences*, and their stimulus meanings may without fear of contradiction be said to do full justice to their meanings (1960, 42).

Quine grants that the difference between an occasion sentence that is an observation sentence, and one that is not, is a matter of degree. "What we have is a gradation of observationality from one extreme, at 'Red' or above, to the other extreme at 'Bachelor' or below" (1960, 42). And

> ...in behavioral terms, an occasion sentence may be said to be the more observational the more nearly its stimulus meanings for different speakers tend to coincide (1960, 43).

For Quine's immediate predecessors as well as for many of his contemporaries, individual sentences are the bearers of empirical content, and primary among them are observation sentences–sentences whose truth or falsity can be determined by some form of simple, direct perception and which together constitute the check points of science. We have just seen that Quine does have his own notion of observation sentences. And Quine believes it can play much of the role scientists and philosophers of science have traditionally taken observation sentences to play:

> To philosophers 'observation sentence' suggests the datum sentences of science. On this score our version is not amiss; for the observation sentences as we have identified them are just the occasion sentences on which there is pretty sure to be firm agreement on the part of well-placed observers. Thus they are just the sentences on which a scientist will tend to fall back when pressed by doubting colleagues.

This seems fair enough. But this passage continues thus:

> Moreover, the philosophical doctrine of infallibility of observation sentences is sustained under our version. For there is scope for error and dispute only insofar as the connections with experience whereby sentences are appraised are multifarious and indirect, mediated through time by theory in conflicting ways; there is none insofar as verdicts to a sentence are directly keyed to present stimulation. (This

46

immunity to error is, however, like observationality itself, for us a matter of degree.) Our version of observation sentences departs from a philosophical tradition in allowing the sentences to be about ordinary things instead of requiring them to report sense data, but this departure has not lacked proponents (1960, 44).

We can certainly grant the first claim of the extended passage just quoted–that Quine's observation sentences play the role traditional observation sentences were intended to play, that of being the sentences on which scientists fall back when challenged. But the claim that they are "infallible" is harder to accept.

Recall that in developing his notion of an observation sentence, Quine presumes our full knowledge of physiology, anatomy, neurology, (and much more)–for he needs the findings of these disciplines to develop a workable notion of sensory stimulation of a person ("the temporally ordered set of all those of his exteroceptors that are triggered on that occasion"). Without a theory of sensory stimulation Quine could not develop his notions of stimulus meaning and stimulus synonymy. Quine also needs at least the basics of stimulus-response psychology as support for his notion of language learning and of stimulus meaning. This is holism at work. The triggerings of exteroceptors are as much posits as are the denizens of sub-molecular space. The notion of an observation sentence is, as a result, thoroughly theory laden. So observation sentences, construed holophrastically, are infallible or immune to error only to the extent one has confidence in and accepts all of the theory that lies behind Quine's account of observation sentences and of stimulation. The bodies of scientific theory in question tell us, if you will, that there is little room for error in observation sentences, and empirical content spreads from such sentences across the whole of our theory of nature. So observation sentences are as reliable as the theories they support and are supported by. Another way to put this is to say that if our best going theories, or at least those used to construct Quine's notions of experience and of observation sentences, are correct, then observation sentences are at least largely immune to error. Our theory of the world tells us that these sentences carry the "unvarnished news" empiricists have sought.

Quine is using all of this machinery of science to reconstitute empiricism. As we are recounting the effort, he has thus far reconstituted the core notion of early and mid 20th century empiricism, the observation sentence. This is a major achievement. But note that so far observation sentences are being construed holophrastically. We do not yet have an account either of how sentences construed normally, non-holophrastically, have empirical content, or of how the empirical content firmly located in observation sentences spreads through our entire theory of the world, including mathematics and logic. We have not yet explicated how Quine gets from observation sentences construed holophrastically to observation sentences that are, as he claims in the above passage, "about ordinary things."

Quine deals with the move from one-word sentences to sentences as composed of multiple words in both the context of infants learning language and that of the field linguist constructing a translation manual. He believes each of us learned some words as one word sentences, and others "contextually, or by abstraction" as fragments of sentences learned as wholes (1960, 14). At some point in the process, multi-word sentences that were originally learned as one-word sentences come to be seen as multi-word. Observation sentences come to be non-holophrastic and "about" ordinary things. For the linguist, as for the infant, a threshold event is the mastering of the mechanisms of individuation. That 'Gavagai' and 'Rabbit', as sentences, are stimulus synonymous (or nearly enough so) does not mean that as terms they denote the same things (rabbits).

> For, consider 'gavagai'. Who knows but that the objects to which this term applies are not rabbits after all, but mere stages, or brief temporal segments, of rabbits? In either event the stimulus situations that prompt assent to 'Gavagai' would be the same as for 'Rabbit'. Or perhaps the objects to which 'gavagai' applies are all the sundry undetached parts of rabbits; again the stimulus meaning would register no difference (1960, 51-52).

What the linguist needs is the machinery of individuation of her informant's language, the machinery of same and different:

> Nothing not distinguished in stimulus meaning itself is to be distinguished by pointing, unless the pointing is accompanied by questions of identity and diversity: 'Is this the same gavagai as that?', 'Do we have here one gavagai or two?' (1960, 53).

Similarly, the infant has not mastered individuation until he or she has learned to use 'mama again' and 'more water' and has rejected 'more mama' and 'water again'. The resources of stimulus-response theory are not adequate to yield a mastery of these and other mechanisms of individuation. The linguist solves the problem by importing her own conceptual scheme (one of physical objects, including rabbits, rather than one of events or undetached rabbit parts) to the members of the community she is studying. The infant solves the problem by aping the linguistic behavior of its community.

Quine takes the empirical content of observation sentences construed holophrastically to carry over to those same sentences construed as containing multiple words. And this is how empirical content carries over to theoretical sentences:

> Component words [of sentences conceived of holophrastically] are there merely as component syllables, theory-free. But these words recur in theoretical contexts in the fullness of time. It is precisely this sharing of words, by observation sentences and theoretical sentences, that provides logical connections between the two kinds of sentences and makes observation relevant to scientific theory. Retrospectively those once innocent observation sentences are theory-laden indeed (1990b, 7).

In *Pursuit of Truth* Quine also tries to clarify the notion of empirical content. To do so he introduces the notion of an observation categorical.

> A generality that is compounded of observables in this way–'Whenever this, that'–is what I call an observation categorical. It is compounded of observation sentences (10).

Examples of observation categoricals are

> Whenever smoke, fire.
> Whenever snow, white.
> Whenever mama, food.

Each is compounded of two observation sentences, in these cases of two one-word observation sentences. Observation categoricals are themselves standing sentences (for a given speaker, they will always be assented to or never assented to). A refined version of the observation categorical is the *focal* observation categorical, *e.g.*,

> Whenever there is a raven, it is black.
> When a willow grows at the water's edge, it leans over the water.

These differ from simple observation categoricals because there is pronominal cross reference from the second observation sentence back to the first, requiring that both component sentences be construed non-holophrastically.

Quine holds that it is through observation categoricals that science is put to the test. "The observational test of scientific hypotheses... and indeed of sentences generally, consists in testing observation categoricals that they imply" (1990b,12). He goes on to give the following "deceptively precise but withal instructive definition of empirical content":

> Call an observation categorical *analytic* for a given speaker if, as in 'Robins are birds', the affirmative stimulus meaning for him of the one component is included in that of the other. Otherwise *synthetic*. Call a sentence or set of sentences *testable* if it implies some synthetic observation categoricals. Call two observation categoricals *synonymous* if their respective components have the same stimulus meanings. Then the *empirical content* of a testable sentence or set of sentences for that speaker is the set of all the synthetic observation categoricals that it implies, plus all synonymous ones (1990b, 17).

Quine next explicitly notes the implications of holism.

> Some unconjoined single sentences qualify as testable, notably the synthetic observation categoricals themselves. For the most part, however, a testable set or conjunction of sentences has to be pretty big, and such is the burden of holism. It is a question of critical semantic mass (1990b, 17).

To what extent has Quine reconstituted empiricism? Narrowly construed, we have a doctrine of observation sentences. For each speaker, some of these are learned holophrastically. For a given language, wordhood comes about however it does and each of us learns to see sentences, first construed holophrastically, as consisting of multiple individual words. By analogy and context we learn other words and other observation sentences, not construed holophrastically. We have not only the notion of an observation sentence, but also limited versions of the analytic/synthetic distinction and of synonymy (limited to observation sentences and observation categoricals). And this meager input is, our best going theories tell us, the material from which we have, over the ages, constructed our best going theories. Our theories evolve and come to allow us to explain and predict future sensory experiences. A key vehicle in the process is the observation categorical. The empirical content, that is meaning, of whatever chunk of science one might take, for a given speaker, is the set of synthetic observation categoricals implied by that chunk of science. The empirical content of the observation categoricals is the content of their component observation sentences, and in the end the content of these sentences is the triggerings of exteroceptors. At levels above that of observation categoricals, what is important is what sentences are implied by what sets of sentences. Theories are to be formulated, revised, and abandoned on grounds of which observational categoricals they imply (and of how simple and unified and so forth they are). What posits we take our theories to require does not seem to enter into this discussion. But more on this in the next chapter.

By now, readers may be wondering if there isn't some tension among the views outlined in this chapter and those of the preceding two. Holism, as earlier described, would seem to dictate that the relationship between experience (the triggerings of our exteroceptors) and the theories we maintain about macro and microscopic objects and events, is complex and indirect. It also would seem to dictate that the associations of specific stimulus conditions with a particular observation sentence or observation categorical are themselves partly determined by bodies of theory. Do observation sentences and observational categoricals, as just defined, "cut through" the web of language and accepted theories that holism assumes? Do they restore a simple and direct connection between the triggerings of our sensory receptors and the theories we build?

It is an obvious implication of holism that when an observation sentences "falsifies" an observation categorical yielded by a body of theory, we will have "much latitude of choice" in determining *which* sentence or sentences of the theory that implied the categorical (whether we consider some "modest chunk" of theory or some substantial part of our largest theory of nature) is or are in need of revision. So, too, as Quine notes in "Five Milestones of Empiricism," citing a similar argument offered by Duhem, when we choose to treat one sentence of a theory "as vulnerable," we have also chosen "to treat... the rest, for the time being, as firm" (1981e, 71). Finally, the experiential situations a scientist associates with an observation sentence is in part determined by the bodies of theory he or she has learned. Similarly, we may well come to associate smoke with fire, snow with white, and so forth; but these associations are made on the basis of an inherited body of theory in which smoke, fire, snow, and white figure.

If this is correct, then the theory of science that Quine is working to develop remains a far cry from an epistemology that could serve to answer the skeptic. When we engage in epistemology as Quine envisions it, we work, as always, "from within."

> It is by thinking within this unitary conceptual scheme itself, thinking about the processes of the physical world, that we come to appreciate that the world can be evidenced only through stimulation of our senses...

51

Epistemology, so conceived, continues to probe the sensory evidence for discourse about the world; but it no longer seeks to relate such discourse somehow to an imaginary and impossible sense-datum language. Rather it faces the fact that society teaches us our physicalistic language by training us to associate various physicalistic sentences directly, in multifarious ways, with irritations of our sensory surfaces, and by training us also to associate various such sentences with one another (1966g, 239-240).

Holism remains intact.

Alternatively said, the situation may be this. Quine takes two paths in his explorations of the relationship between our experiences (construed as triggerings of exteroceptors) and our theories. One starts with the identification of the kind of sentence (that kind first learned as a whole, before one has caught on to physical object theory) that can be said to be directly associated with sensory stimulations. In identifying this kind of sentence Quine uses our going theories of language and language learning. The other path starts with sentences that clearly do not have their own isolatable empirical content, that are associated with stimulus conditions only as parts of larger bodies of theory that together "face the tribunal of experience." The less theoretical of these contain words that also occur within sentences of the former sort construed holophrastically. These in turn contain words that also occur in more theoretical sentences, and so on to the most abstract and theoretical parts of science. In this way Quine hopes the two paths meet, and the empirical content directly associated with observation sentences and observation categoricals spreads through the entire reach of our theories.[4] Whether Quine has succeeded in bridging the gap between the most abstract and theoretical of discourse with the most concrete of observation sentences is perhaps an open question. If he has not, it is clearly a project that needs to be completed, completed by working within our ongoing theories and by using all the applicable findings of those theories.

Endnotes

[1] "Empirical Content," 24-25.

[2] *Word and Object*, 10.

[3] Quine does not hold that 'Gavagai' and 'Rabbit' have exactly the same stimulus meaning, in part because he grants that it will be impossible to strip away all collateral information available to the linguist's informant. "The fact is that ...[the linguist] ...translates not by

identity of stimulus meanings, but by significant approximation of stimulus meanings" (1960, 40).

[4] Quine thinks well of contextual definitions–definitions that explain a word by specifying all the contexts (sentences) in which the word can be correctly used. The view behind contextual definitions is that if one knows all the contexts in which a word can be used, one knows everything there is to know about the meaning of the word, even if one cannot "say" in a single sentence what the word means. Contextual definition may be a key tool, for Quine, in bridging the apparent gap between full blown theories and observation sentences.

6

What There Is

"The time has come", the Walrus said,
"To talk of many things:
Of shoes–and ships–and sealing-
wax–
Of cabbages–and kings–
And why the sea is boiling hot–
And whether pigs have wings."

– Lewis Carroll[1]

Ontological Commitments

Science, it would certainly appear, is concerned with discovering both what there is and how the things that are behave, *i.e.*, it is concerned with discovering and explaining the nature and workings of the world. Quine holds that philosophy of science is science gone self-conscious; so it is to be expected that Quine would address, not what there is, but how science arrives at and defends its claims as to what there is, its ontological commitments. And this is in fact the case. Quine discusses the nature of science's ontological commitments in many of his writings, and in these he often construes science broadly to include both common sense and (parts of) philosophy. We begin with two fairly early essays, "On What There Is" and "Posits and Reality." These are among the richest, best crafted, and most accessible of Quine's essays.

The opening paragraph of "On What There Is" is classic Quine:

A curious thing about the ontological problem is its simplicity. It can be put in three Anglo-Saxon monosyllables: 'What is there?' It can be answered, moreover, in a word– 'Everything'–and everyone will accept this answer as true. However, this is merely to say that there is what there is.

There remains room for disagreement over cases; and so the issue has stayed alive down the centuries (1).

In the course of the next twenty pages, Quine exposes the folly of distinguishing between existence and being, the bizarre consequences of using modal terms ('possible' and 'necessary') as adjectives attaching to nouns and noun phrases rather than to sentences as wholes, and the folly of a blanket acceptance of platonism (universals). "On What There Is" is not a defense of physicalism or any general metaphysical position. Nor is it an attack on the notion of meanings as non-linguistic (and perhaps mental) entities, or on abstract entities generally. The real topic of this essay is that of how we, through the language we use and theories we generate, do and do not acquire ontological commitments–do and do not become committed to the existence of specific things and kinds of thing.

It is in this essay that Quine introduces the view that ontological commitment is carried, not by names and definite descriptions, but by what is said of some or every thing. That is, ontological commitment is carried by the general terms (what Quine calls the "ideology") of natural language, coupled with the apparatus of pronouns and quantity terms (whose analogues are the predicates, variables, and quantifiers of formal theories). At its end, we do not know what there is (or what Quine thinks there is), except in the sense that there is what there is (everything). But we *do* know what it is for a theory, and we as holders of a theory, to be committed to there being this or that thing or kind of thing.

Quine devotes the first pages to an exploration of the view (not his own) that whatever we speak of, even by way of denying its existence (as in 'Pegasus does not exist'), must, in virtue of our speaking *of* it, exist or have some kind of ontological status (being, subsistence...). For example, if Pegasus did not have some kind of ontological status, how could we coherently say of Pegasus that it does not exist?

> This is the old Platonic riddle of nonbeing. Nonbeing must in some sense be, otherwise what is it that there is not? This tangled doctrine might be nicknamed *Plato's beard;* historically it has proved tough, frequently dulling the edge of Occam's razor (1-2).

If we assume that every occurrence of a name or other singular term must have meaning for the sentence within which it occurs to be meaningful, and we take meaning, at least for singular terms, to be reference, then if 'Pegasus does not exist' is to be meaningful,

'Pegasus' must refer to something. Since there is no flesh and blood winged horse about for it to refer to, the temptation of Quine's philosopher McX is to presume it refers to an idea in our heads. On the other hand, Wyman, Quine's second theorist, concludes that Pegasus, while failing to exist, does "subsist," does have "being as an unactualized possible" (2-3).

Both views, Quine demonstrates, are problematic. Winged horses presumably both fly and eat oats. McX's ideas do neither. And Wyman's allowance of unactualized possibles opens the door to an "overpopulated universe" that is

> ...in many ways unlovely. It offends the aesthetic sense of us who have a taste for desert landscapes, but this is not the worst of it. Wyman's slum of possibles is a breeding ground for disorderly elements. Take, for instance, the possible fat man in the doorway; and, again, the possible thin man in the doorway. Are they the same possible man, or two possible men? How do we decide? How many possible men are there in the doorway? Are there more possible thin ones than fat ones? ...We'd be better simply to clear Wyman's slum and be done with it (4).

And, in fact, we have need neither of McX's mental ideas nor of Wyman's unactualized possibles. We can do without both by dispensing with names (and singular terms generally). Bertrand Russell's theory of descriptions provides a way of eliminating definite descriptions (what Quine calls "singular descriptions"), *i.e.*, of eliminating phrases that purport to identify exactly one thing, in favor of somewhat complicated existential claims. For example, 'The author of *Waverley* was a poet' can be paraphrased as

> Something wrote *Waverley* and was a poet and nothing else wrote *Waverley* (6).

Here, Quine notes,

> the burden of objective reference which had been put upon the descriptive phrase ['the author of *Waverley*'] is now taken over by words of the kind that logicians call bound variables, variables of quantification, namely, words like 'something', 'nothing', 'everything' (6).

Note that statements of the sort 'Something is thus-and-so' and 'Everything is thus-and-so' are not of the subject/predicate form. Neither 'something' nor 'everything' nor 'nothing' is a name of anything. So the question of whether the subject term refers is moot. There is no subject term.

Having eliminated definite descriptions, we can now eliminate names, provided we can first turn them into definite descriptions. And this is straightforward. To eliminate the name 'Pegasus', for example,

> We have only to rephrase 'Pegasus' as a description, in any way that seems adequately to single out our idea; say, 'the winged horse that was captured by Bellerophon' (7).

This device allows us to transfer the "meaning" of names to predicates while eliminating the names themselves, and thus the question of whether they do or do not refer. In making this move Quine does assumes that the work a name does can be done equally well by descriptions that purport to single out the entity the name purports to refer to[2]–whether or not they have reference.[3] Accepting these two presuppositions, we can

> proceed to analyze the statement 'Pegasus is', or 'Pegasus is not', precisely on the analogy of Russell's analysis of 'The author of Waverley is' and 'The author of Waverley is not' (7).

And we get rid of 'Pegasus does not exist' in favor of

> It is not the case that there is something that is a winged horse and was captured by Bellerophon and is such that nothing else is a winged horse and was captured by Bellerophon.

By the same procedure we can, of course, eliminate 'Bellerophon'.

Having shown that names and definite descriptions are, in principle, eliminable, we are now in a position to discuss existential issues, *e.g.*, whether there are universals, or attributes, or classes, or meanings, without begging the question in favor of their existence.

> We can very easily involve ourselves in ontological commitments by saying, for example, that *there is something* (bound variable) which red houses and sunsets have in common; or that *there is something* which is a prime number larger than a million (12).

But we are not forced, by the mere structure of language, to make such commitments. Quine himself, of course, demurs to make the first ontological commitment but is quite happy to make the second. In general terms, Quine's view is that while we must admit some abstract entities, *e.g.*, classes or sets, we need not accept universals generally.

It is, to our knowledge, in "On What There Is" that the phrase "To be is to be the value of a variable" first appears in Quine's writings.

This phrase gained currency as characterizing Quine's view of what there is, despite the fact that he explicitly notes in this essay that it does not.

> We look to bound variables in connection with ontology not in order to know what there is, but in order to know what a given remark or doctrine, ours or someone else's, *says* there is; and this much is quite properly a problem involving language. But what there is is another question (15-16).

Here Quine does not mean to suggest that the first question cannot be answered or is even difficult to answer. It is a question for science, broadly construed, to answer. What there is, or at least what we take there to be, is what our most serious theory of nature says there is–what must be taken as the value of the variables of this theory in order for its claims to be true. There seems to be no hint here of what is to come–the inscrutability of reference and the indeterminacy of translation, doctrines to which we turn in the next chapter.

With the elimination of singular terms (names and definite descriptions), one form of reference is also eliminated (reference as the relation between a name and the thing named). But reference remains in at least two other senses. The first concerns the role of bound variables of quantification and their analogues in natural language:

> the burden of objective reference which has been put upon the descriptive phrase ['the author of *Waverley*'] is now taken over by words of the kind that logicians call bound variables, variables of quantification, namely, words like 'something', 'nothing', 'everything'. These words, far from purporting to be names specifically of the author of *Waverley*, do not purport to be names at all; they refer to entities generally, with a kind of studied ambiguity peculiar to themselves (6).

The claim that bound variables "refer to entities generally with a kind of studied ambiguity peculiar to themselves" needs explication. It is this. Most of us tend to think of claims such as "Horses are mammals" and "The author of *Word and Object* is in the audience" as being about, or referring to, respectively, horses and Quine. But this is not so; at least it is not so on Quine's preferred renderings of these sentences, *i.e.*,

> each thing is such that if it is a horse then it is a mammal

for the first and

> there is at least one thing that is the author of *Word and Object*, and nothing else is the author, and that thing is in the audience

for the second. So construed, 'horses are mammals' is arguably about each thing in the domain, for it says of each such thing that *if* it is a horse, *then* it is a mammal. This claim does tell us something about each member of the domain. This is the "studied ambiguity" Quine talks of. Similarly, 'The author of *Word and Object* is in the audience' does not pick out Quine and say of him that he is in the audience. (If it functioned so, it would be meaningless when said of audiences lacking Quine.) Rather, it says, of the members of the domain, that one of them is the author of *Word and Object* and is in the audience. When Quine is absent it is thus false but meaningful. In both cases, it is all the members of the domain that the sentences are "about"; hence, Quine's claim that the variables of quantification "refer to entities generally with a kind of studied ambiguity peculiar to themselves."

In any event, despite all of his talk about reference–of bound variables referring to entities "with a studied ambiguity" and of referential position, reference is not a semantic notion essential to Quine's understanding of theories and things. Predication is. That is to say, Quine rejects the view that our theories and we are connected to the world through names and acts of naming. He argues, instead, that it is by the ascription of predicates to something or everything–or, in the language of formal logic, through claims that something, or everything, satisfies an open sentence–that we and the theories we accept come to have ontological commitments. It is not 'Scott', but acceptance of 'is an author of such-and-such a sort' as being true of something, that commits us to the existence of Scott (where 'author of such-and-such a sort' is a unique specification of Scott). We cannot "determine separately what to talk about and what to say about it" (1960, 38). Contrary to *Genesis*, naming could not have been Adam's first linguistic task. This elimination of reference in favor of predication, or better in favor of satisfaction of open sentences, is, we will later see, part of what leads Quine to the doctrine of the inscrutability of reference. But we are getting ahead of ourselves.

The argument of "On What There Is" is that we are ontologically committed to those entities that must be part of the domain of our theory in order for the sentences of the theory to be true. So what we are committed to depends on what theory we accept. What theory should we accept? In "Posits and Reality" Quine explores the relations among what might appear to be three quite separate theories: our everyday theory of macro objects, the theory of physicists with its domain of molecules, atoms, and subatomic particles, and the theory of the epistemologist with its sense-data or surrogates therefore. Several views are possible here. One is that either macro objects, or micro

59

objects, or sense data, are real–but not more than one of these three kinds of objects are real. This is decidedly not Quine's view. He argues, as the title of the article suggests, that macro objects (chairs, trees, and planets), micro objects (molecules, atoms, and subatomic particles), and sensory objects (sense data or surrogates therefore) are all posits. In *Word and Object* Quine is explicit that "To call a posit a posit is not to patronize it..."

> Everything to which we concede existence is a posit from the standpoint of a description of the theory-building process, and simultaneously real from the standpoint of the theory that is being built. Nor let us look down on the standpoint of the theory as make-believe; for we can never do better than occupy the standpoint of some theory or other, the best we can muster at the time.
>
> What reality is like is the business of scientists, in the broadest sense, painstakingly to surmise; and what there is, what is real, is part of the question (22).

In "Posits and Reality" Quine also claims that each of the three kinds of posits discussed above is fundamental in its own way:

> Sense data, [if they are to be posited at all], are *evidentially* fundamental: every man is beholden to his senses for every hint of bodes. The physical particles are *naturally* fundamental, in this kind of way: laws of behavior of those particles afford, so far as we know, the simplest formulation of a general theory of what happens. Common-sense bodies, finally, are *conceptually* fundamental: it is by reference to them that the concepts which have to do with physical particles or even with sense data tend to be framed and phrased (1966g, 239).

So perhaps Quine's view is that we have three theories and that what is real is relative to the theory from or within which we are speaking. This is what the passage from *Word and Object* quoted above might suggest if we assume there are real boundaries between common sense theories, physics, and epistemology. We move among the theories, changing our stance, as the occasion demands. Each kind of thing is real from within the theory that posits it. But this is not Quine's view. The just quoted passage from "Posits and Reality" continues thus:

> But these three types of priority must not be viewed as somehow determining three competing, self-sufficient conceptual schemes. Our one serious conceptual scheme is the

inclusive, evolving one of science, which we inherit and, in our several small ways, help to improve (239).

And in *Word and Object* Quine asks

> Have we now so far lowered our sights as to settle for a relativistic doctrine of truth–rating the statements of each theory as true for that theory, and brooking no higher criticism?

His answer is

> Not so. The saving consideration is that we continue to take seriously our own particular aggregate science, our own particular world-theory or loose total fabric of quasi-theories, whatever it may be. Unlike Descartes, we own and use our beliefs of the moment, even in the midst of philosophizing, until by what is vaguely called scientific method we change them here and there for the better. Within our own total evolving doctrine, we can judge truth as earnestly and absolutely as can be; subject to correction, but that goes without saying (24-25).

This suggests that our serious, inclusive, theory countenances the objects of common sense, the micro objects of physics, the objects of chemistry, biology, geology and so forth, and if not sense data then some surrogate for them. From the standpoint of this, our present theory, we judge all real and each fundamental in its own way. This picture is quite attractive. Posits are the best we can do by way of saying what there is, just as theories are the best we can do by way of saying what is true.

But Quine's views on posits are not quite this simple, as we begin to explore in the next two sections and in Chapter 7.

Physicalism and Reductionism

The world, even Quine's own desert landscape, seems awash in objects–DNA molecules, cultures, ecosystems, organizations, cells, intelligent systems, gases, species, political parties, equations, radio waves, neurons, oceans, social movements, artifacts, organisms, hormones, geological formations, behaviors, and subatomic particles, to name just a few. Stretch the ontological net to the universe and there are more objects besides–galaxies, supernovae, and black holes among the more splendid.

These and a host of other objects populate the domains and theories of the various sciences, and, to a greater or lesser extent (depending on whose "common sense" we consult), common sense theories as well. There are, of course, differences among them. Some (*e.g.*, subatomic particles) are too small to directly observe; of some (*e.g.*, electrons) we are told that our very observing them changes them; of some (such as stars) we only observe their past; of some (such as extinct species and past civilizations) we only observe traces of the changes they wrought; and, of some (like the Milky Way), it is unlikely that we will enjoy a full view in the near term, if ever.

The objects of our world and universe also differ in what we might call their "compounded-ness." By current lights, the most fundamental or elementary objects are studied in particle or field physics; those of other branches of physics and of chemistry are a rung up on the ladder of complexity; and those of biology up yet another rung. In between these rungs, bio-physics and biochemistry find their place, and somewhere on the ladder we fit astronomy, astro-biology, and geology. Rungs intermediate to those noted mark off specialties within specific sciences (the objects in the domain of molecular biology, for example, are more fundamental than those of endocrinology). Psychology (at least empirical psychology) seems a rung above biology, although there are "cross overs" in domains (for example, in neuro endocrinology). Higher still are the various social sciences (anthropology, sociology, archaeology, linguistics, economics, political science, and so forth), for the objects which figure in their domains (political societies, nations, social organizations, cultures and so on) are more composite than those which figure in chemistry and at least some of biology. At least so says our present theory of the world.

We note three things about our vertical ladder. First, even if we assume that, by virtue of the differences in their domains, the various sciences are to some degree autonomous, our current understanding of how things work dictate that there are constraints which flow upward. For example, biology dictates that humans won't fly without aid of jet engines or parachutes, even if wanting to do so should turn out to be built-in to human psychology. And in general, the objects and events posited at any level on the ladder–be they periods of geological change, civil rights movements, episodes of speciation, or economic cycles–are subject to the laws of physics.

The second thing to note about the ladder so far described is the absence (with the exception of whatever the most elementary objects turn out to be) of objects about which it doesn't seem to make sense to talk of "component parts"–and certainly not, some would have it, of "physical parts." Yet a host of such objects–minds, thoughts, ideas, and beliefs among the more notable–seem to abound, and with great consequence. There are two ways we might try to accommodate minds, beliefs, and their ilk. We might just add them–as indivisible, non-physical objects–to the domains of whatever sciences seem to require them, and swell the ranks of the ontology of our overall theory of nature to include a class of objects different from any other and, so to speak, "free floating." Alternatively, we might think it a reasonable hypothesis (until shown otherwise) that minds, beliefs, ideas and their ilk, are, in the end, physical states of physical objects (us), not different in kind from other physical states. Then we might seek to learn about these physical states–in, say, one or more of the neurosciences, evolutionary biology, and so forth. Is one route better than the other? This question involves us, of course, in ontological decision-making, a topic to be taken up shortly.

The third thing to note about the objects which populate the theories of the various sciences, common-sense, and epistemology is that for all the differences in their degree of "compounded-ness," all are real–at least all that are respectable and posited by theories that allow us to explain and predict some of what happens.

Or so it would seem.

Why 'Or so it would seem'? We begin our consideration of this question by exploring Quine's most general metaphysical commitment, physicalism, and another empiricist doctrine of the logico-empiricist tradition he inherited, reductionism. On the basis of the first commitment Quine has been understood to be committed to versions of reductionism. We here try to set things straight, or at least straighter.

Three assumptions outlined in the last several pages–that the plethora of objects which many of the sciences study can be seen as constituted by more elementary objects, that there is a domain of objects that is most fundamental, and that we should evaluate ontological commitments–came together in empiricist philosophy of science of the 1950s in the form of "unity of science" theses. We here consider metaphysical unity theses, which assume or envision a unity among (or eventual unification of) the various ontologies and laws propounded in the various sciences. Metaphysical unity theses are termed "reductionist" (often pejoratively) because they are understood to assume (or prescribe) that the ontologies, laws, and explanations of all the other "mature sciences" can be "reduced to" the ontologies, laws, and explanations of physics. For reasons considered in earlier chapters, the reduction envisioned involves translating the sentences of one science (say, biology) into another (say, chemistry) whose objects belong to the next lower level. A relatively weak version of metaphysical unity, already mentioned, is that whatever the domain of a particular science (with the exception of those fields in physics which study the most elementary objects), these objects are made up of still more elementary objects–objects studied by a science "lower" on the ladder. A stronger version is that for some thing *to count* as an object, it must be such that it could be "reduced," via a series of micro reductions (one science at a time), to the most elementary objects. To see why this is a stronger thesis, consider the objects we earlier found difficult to locate on our vertical ladder–minds, thoughts, beliefs, and the like. This second thesis would suggest that, if these are unable to be reduced in the ways just outlined, they don't (or shouldn't) *count* as objects or events. The strongest version of metaphysical unity is the thesis that the objects which figure in the most fundamental science (at present, physics) are "more real" than those studied by other sciences.[4] We have seen in the preceding section that the strongest of these theses does not seem to be Quine's view. We turn now to Quine's most general metaphysical commitment, physicalism, and explore whether this commitment entails reductionism of some sort.

In "Facts of the Matter," Quine offers a formulation of physicalism which he describes as incomplete. His formulation makes no mention of objects at all, because Quine takes the shift in physics from particle models to field theory as "severing" the link with physical objects in "our most refined theory." Thus, Quine defines making a difference in matters of fact, *i.e.*, he defines the thesis of physicalism, without reference to bodies.

> To profess materialism after [the shift to field theory] would seem grotesquely inappropriate; but physicalism, reasonably reformulated, retains its vigor and validation... What now is the claim of physicalism? Simply that there is no difference in matters of fact without a difference in the fulfillment of the physical-state predicates by space-time regions (165-66).

This is not to say that only those things that make for a difference in the fulfillment of the physical-state predicates by space-time regions are real. Mathematical objects, sets or classes, are real (for Quine) though they make no difference in matters of fact so specified. And so stated, physicalism would seem to come to no more than the ruling out of "non-physical" entities alleged to make a difference in "matters of fact." Unless we are committed to the existence of such entities (for example, souls), the thesis is minimal and, for many of us, non-controversial. A more interesting issue is whether physicalism is, or commits us to, reductionism.

Sometimes, it is best to begin with the punch line. There is, we suggest, an interesting kind of reductionism attributable to Quine, and it has two aspects. First, physicalism dictates that at whatever level we are describing changes or states in matters of fact (in sociology, chemistry, biology, common sense, and so forth), the sentences of our theory need to be able to be expressed–*in principle*–in sentences concerning only the fulfillment of place-time regions. We emphasize 'in principle' to underscore that we may not be interested enough to undertake any such translation. Second, and this we submit is the interesting thesis, it is the in principle possibility of translating sentences of some theory into sentences that only concern the fulfillment of physical-state predicates by space-time regions, that *finances*–in the sense of "underwriting" or "legitimating"–its ontological commitments. We know, in Quine's words, "that we are not just bandying about words" (1978, 167) when it is clear that the objects posited by some theory would make a difference in terms of the elementary physical states. This is not to say that physics explains everything. Given holism, it is the whole of science that explains, *i.e.*, the whole of science that bridges sensory stimulations, each part of the fabric supported by the rest. It *is* to say that it would be surprising, given our current understandings of things, if at a fictional end of inquiry in which we understood all of physics, we found ourselves *in principle* unable to predict chemistry.

What are the consequences of physicalism and reductionism as so far described? Quine's views about "mental objects" are particularly instructive. We have noted that Quine is loath to grant ontological status to "mental objects," and that he recommends interpreting mentalistic idiom in behaviorist terms. But the assumption that he writes off mental objects as unimportant obscures more than it illuminates. Quine has consistently maintained that the objects posited in mentalistic idiom–minds, thoughts, ideas, beliefs, and the like–are an appropriate subject of study but as yet too unclarified to function in explanations (1966e and 1981g). The notion of clarification at work here includes the difficulties associated with providing clear identity criteria for mental objects–and Quine, we have seen, takes clarity of identity criteria to be a minimum for ontological admissibility. Quine thus recommends that behaviors are a way of determining and individuating such objects, not that behaviors *are* mental states (whatever such states turn out to be). We can keep and use belief talk to the extent that behaviors *legitimate or underwrite* such talk, and behaviors do so in two ways: they enable us to identify and individuate beliefs, and they do ultimately involve facts of the matter.

Mental states and events do not reduce to behavior, nor are they explained by behavior. They are explained by neurology, when they are explained. But their behavioral adjuncts serve to specify them objectively. When we talk of mental states or events subject to behavioral criteria, we can rest assured that we are not just bandying worlds; there is a physical fact of the matter, a fact ultimately of elementary physical states (1978, 167).

Thus, Quine's turn to behavior and the possibility of eventually explaining behavior via neuroscience is motivated by physicalism and the sort of reductionism he takes physicalism to entail. It is the possibility that our talk of mental states and events could, *in principle*, be expressed in the terms of physiology, and ultimately in terms of elementary physical states, that underwrites our talk of "ideas" and "beliefs." The notion of "explanation" at work in the passage just quoted is that the possibility of "reductively reinterpreting" talk of behaviors in terms of neurophysiology that finances our talk of mental states.

Two last points about physicalism. Quine takes this broad metaphysical commitment to be an implication of our best going theories of the world, not a "first principle." And, like any empirical hypothesis, physicalism is not above revision.

Posits

In the first section of this chapter, we cited several passages which suggest that it is Quine's view that our inclusive theory of nature countenances the objects of common sense, the micro objects of physics (and micro and macro objects of the other sciences), and if not sense data then some surrogate for them. We noted that this picture is an attractive one, but also that Quine's views about posits are not quite so simple. We hope it is by now clear that Quine approaches the ontologies of physics, other sciences, commonsense, and (respectable) epistemology even handedly. We now return to the question of what it means to call the objects of all of these various theories "posits."

Early in "Posits and Reality" Quine entertains the instrumentalist's suggestion that once our theory of molecules and atoms and subatomic particles has been articulated, we can dispense with the objects of that theory "but retain the surrounding ring of derivative laws, thus not disturbing the observable consequences" (235). He rejects this suggestion as not really being "an intelligible possibility" (234). It is not an intelligible suggestion, not because the posits of molecular and atomic theory are essential to the theory, but because *"there is no substantive doctrine of molecules to delete..."*

> The sentences which seem to propound molecules are just devices for organizing the significant sentences of physical theory. No matter if physics makes molecules or other insensible particles seem more fundamental than the objects of common sense; the particles are posited for the sake of a simple physics (237; emphasis added).

So far, Quine's point would seem to be that when we ask "Are molecules *really* real?" we are pushing language beyond its capabilities. To understand why the instrumentalist view is not really an intelligible possibility he suggests we should "reflect upon our words and how we learned them" (235).

> Words are human artifacts, meaningless save as our associating them with experience endows them with meaning. The word 'swarm' is initially meaningful to us through association with such expressions as that of a hovering swarm of gnats, or a swarm of dust motes in a shaft of sunlight. When we extend the word to desks and the like, we are engaged in drawing an analogy between swarms ordinarily so-called, on the one hand, and desks, *etc.*, on the other. The word 'molecule' is then given meaning derivatively: having conceived of desks analogically as swarms, we imagine molecules as the things the desks are swarms of.
>
> The purported question of fact, the question whether the familiar objects around us are really swarms of subvisible particles in vibration, now begins to waver and dissolve. If the words involved make sense only by analogy, then the only question of fact is the question of how good an analogy there is between the behavior of a desk or the like and the behavior, *e.g.*, of a swarm of gnats. What had seemed a direct bearing of the molecular doctrine upon reality has now dwindled to an analogy (235-236).

Remember that Quine does not have more of a theory of language than a stimulus-response theory of language acquisition. He readily concedes, in fact he seems to insist, that in some important sense all language is metaphor and analogy. It is for this reason that the instrumentalist's suggestion that we can dispense with molecules *et al* once we have constructed our theory is beside the point–there is nothing to reject. Language is metaphorical and analogical, all of it. It is to be evaluated by how well it serves the purpose at hand–be it communication or prediction of the firings of sensory receptors or systematization of findings–not by its ontological commitments, all of which are posits.

But it is now not so clear that to call a posit a posit is *not* to patronize it. To be sure, it is not to patronize it by way of saying it is less firm than some ontological commitment that is not a posit, for there are none of the latter. But Quine does seem to be headed towards the view that the posits of our theories, all of them, are of far less firmness and interest than had first appeared. The inscrutability of reference and the indeterminacy of translation are closing in on us.

Before turning to these theses, we suggest that a reasonable way to put together the view of ontology advocated in *Word and Object*, and those of "Posits and Reality" just explored, is the following. On the one hand, naturalism dictates that we can do no better in determining what there is than to look at our current best science, and holism dictates that we can do nothing other than take our going world theory seriously.

> The scientific system, ontology and all, is a conceptual bridge, linking sensory stimulation to sensory stimulation.
>
> But I also [have] an unswerving belief in external things–people, nerve endings, sticks, stones... Now how is all this robust realism to be reconciled with the barren scene that I have just been depicting? The answer is naturalism: the recognition that it is within science itself, and not in some prior philosophy, that reality is to be identified and described... it is a confusion to suppose that we can stand aloof and recognize all the alternative ontologies as true in their several ways... It is a confusion of truth with evidential support. Truth is immanent, and there is no higher. We must speak from within a theory, albeit any of various (1981a, 21-22).

It is also by thinking within our broadest theory of nature, and engaging in self-conscious science (*i.e.*, epistemology)–*i.e.*, analyzing the theory-building process–that we recognize objects as posits.

> Everything to which we concede existence is a posit from the standpoint of a description of the theory-building process, and simultaneously real from the standpoint of the theory that is being built. Nor let us look down on the standpoint of the theory as make-believe; for we can never do better than occupy the standpoint of some theory or other, the best we can muster at the time (1981a, 22).

Putting all this together we get this. From within our world theory, a host of objects are real. When Quine reflects on the "theory-building process" and seeks to describe it, he takes seriously the view that language is learned initially as one word sentences, sentences appropriately said or assented to in the presence of some particular form of stimulation ('Mama' in the presence of mother). He also takes seriously the view that the goal of the scientist is to construct a theory, a set of sentences, to which truth-values (true) can be attached in ways that help us explain and predict the firings of sensory receptors. The world and language (which is part of the world) come together as whole sentences that are assented to or dissented from in the presence or absence of appropriate stimulations. For the empiricist, reality is in this correlating of sentences and stimulatory situations, not in the objects posited (by analogy) for constituent words to refer to, or for variables to take as values.

In short, "ontology is not what mainly matters" (1978, 64-65). The stage is now set for inscrutability of reference and indeterminacy of translation.

Endnotes

[1] Lewis Carroll, *Through the Looking Glass.*

[2] Since there are generally multiple such descriptions, some will suggest that it is incumbent upon Quine to provide a mechanism for determining which description is to replace a name. (For example, do we replace 'Pegasus' with 'the winged horse that was captured by Bellerophon', or with 'the winged horse that sprang from the blood of the slain Medusa'?) But Quine is under no such obligation. Recall that Quine says "We have only to rephrase 'Pegasus' as a description, *in any way that seems adequately to single out our idea..."* (emphasis added). What description we use, on a given occasion, to replace Pegasus, or any other name, will depend on the purpose of the discourse we are involved in on that occasion.

[3] Quine's view is later rejected by Kripke and his doctrine of rigid designators.

[4] Advocates of such theses typically grant that the envisioned unity of scientific ontologies might not prove feasible. But they take the possibility that the theories of, say, biology might ultimately be shown to derive from those of a science dealing with more (and eventually the most) elementary objects, as a reasonable goal for both science and the philosophy of science.

7

Indeterminacies

Three theses of indeterminacy have figured conspicuously in my writings: indeterminacy of translation, inscrutability of reference and underdetermination of scientific theory. Each... presupposes a distinctive further topic... The topic presupposed by translation is stimulation. The topic presupposed by inscrutability of reference is reification. The topic presupposed by underdetermination of science is empirical content.

–W.V. Quine[1]

We have discussed Quine's holism. It is in every way a salutary doctrine, recommending open-mindedness and cautioning against dogmatism. It uniformly sees the results of reification as posits, and does not demean them for being such. When combined with Quine's naturalism it has room for, and can explain, the dead ends and not-so-promising avenues explored by science as well as the successes of science, all within the bounds of science. It makes clear how and why simplicity, familiarity of principle, scope, fecundity, and the other "cognitive virtues" have an important role to play in theory formulation.[2] And it is part and parcel of Quine's view that theories are underdetermined[3] by evidence.

In Chapter 5 we discussed Quine's reconstruction of empiricism and his account of the empirical content of observation sentences, and derivatively, of all of science. This reconstruction is intimately connected with Quine's theses of the inscrutability of reference and the indeterminacy of translation. We here explore each of these three theses in some detail, as well as the question of what (if any) relationships they bear to one another. We begin with underdetermination, and later return to it in light of the inscrutability of reference and the indeterminacy of translation.

Underdetermination of Theories

Quine is, of course, a Humean. (He quips in "Epistemology Naturalized" that "The Humean predicament is the human predicament," 72.) Past experience is no sure guide to future experience, and therefore theories, the very nature of which it is to predict future experience, are of course in this minimal sense underdetermined by the evidence for them (past experience). But Quine is not a skeptic. He rejects Hume's conclusion that past experience provides no rational basis for predicting future experience.[4] And Quine's thesis of the underdetermination of theories is more interesting than the now familiar Humean point that induction is not deduction.

Quine is a traditional empiricist in the sense that he gives a privileged position to experience or to whatever cleaned-up, made-respectable version of experience he can construct (the triggerings of exteroceptors). Indeed one of the primary concerns in his writings subsequent to "Two Dogmas of Empiricism" has been to come up with a respectable version of sense experience, one that can take the weight empiricists need it to bear. We have already quoted several passages in which Quine expresses his commitment to the epistemic primacy of sense experience and to theories being underdetermined by experience. Here are a few additional such passages:

From "Two Dogmas of Empiricism":

> Total science, mathematical and natural and human, is similarly but more extremely underdetermined by experience [than the posits of physical objects and the algebra of rational and irrational numbers]. The edge of the system must be kept squared with experience; the rest, with all its elaborate myths or fictions, has as its objective the simplicity of laws (45).

From "Things and Their Place in Theories"

> Our talk of external things, our very notion of things, is just a conceptual apparatus that helps us to foresee and control the triggering of our sensory receptors in the light of previous triggerings of our sensory receptors. The triggering, first and last, is all we have to go on (1).

> [It] is a fact of science itself... that science is a conceptual bridge of our own making, linking sensory stimulation to sensory stimulation... (2).

From *Word and Object*

> ...we have no reason to suppose that man's surface irritations even unto eternity admit of any one systematization that is scientifically better or simpler than all possible others. It seems likelier... that countless alternative theories would be tied for first place (23).

From these passages and others it seems fair to conclude that Quine takes theories to be underdetermined in at least three ways in addition to (or as elaborations of) general Humean underdetermination. Sensory experience underdetermines the theory of physical objects, macro, micro, and atomic and sub-atomic, in the sense that there may be (presumably are) alternative posits that would connect past sensory experience with future sensory experience equally well. These alternative posits may be alternative kinds of physical objects, or entities of some other kind entirely, or not entities at all. This is true, but esoteric. Given our actual scientific heritage we are unlikely to abandon our ontology of physical objects for one of events or numbers or whatever. Second, even given our choice of physical objects as the primary constituents of the bridge science affords between past sense experiences and future sense experiences, the details of the bridge are underdetermined by experience. We can redistribute truth-values at will (perversely), or in response to a recalcitrant experience, while retaining our over-all commitment, more or less, to the familiar physical objects and to the bulk of the sentences of our present theory. Finally, our reconstructed notion of sense experience, be it as surface irritations or firings of sensory receptors or the triggerings of exteroceptors, is *itself* a theoretical construct derived from our best going theories (of anatomy, physiology, neurology, and some branches of psychology). This theory of sense experience is itself, like all theories, underdetermined by available evidence (in the above senses). So we could, and future discoveries may lead us to, alter it, and thereby set the stage for a different science connecting, in different ways, our new versions of past sense experiences with our new versions of future sense experiences.

That science is underdetermined in the above ways is, in essence, a re-statement of holism and of the view that reification is a matter of posits, all tentative, some more useful than others. It is an epistemological thesis and speaks to the tentativeness of all of science. There is at least the appearance that one can meaningfully speculate about what an alternative set of posits might be like and how science might be reconstructed around that set of posits. We do not think Quine

72

would demur from any of the foregoing. However, we are far from sure that what we have said so far captures the core of Quine's notion of the underdetermination of theories. But before further pursuing underdetermination it will be useful to have an understanding of two other indeterminacies, the inscrutability of reference and the indeterminacy of translation.

Inscrutability of Reference and Indeterminacy of Translation

The inscrutability of reference and the indeterminacy of translation are elusive theses. Critics and commentators have conflated them with each other, and with the underdetermination of theories. Both theses have been dismissed by some as trivial, and rejected by others as patently false. We hope to do better.

In Chapter 5 we noted that Quine's field linguist is, so long as she treats 'Gavagai' holophrastically and restrains from imposing her own conceptual scheme on that of the Antorians, in no position to hazard a guess as to whether 'gavagai' is a general term taken by the Antorians to be true of rabbits, rabbit-stages, undetached rabbit parts, or rabbithood. In *Pursuit of Truth* Quine says that this case, although involving translation, is an illustration of the inscrutability of reference (which he opines he did not call the 'indeterminacy of reference'), not the indeterminacy of translation.

> Ironically, indeterminacy of translation in the strong sense was not what I coined the word ['Gavagai'] to illustrate. It did not illustrate that, for 'Gavagai' is an observation sentence, firmly translatable holophrastically as '(Lo, a) rabbit'. But this translation is insufficient to fix the reference of 'gavagai' as a term; that was the point of the example. It is an extreme example of the indeterminacy [*aka* inscrutability] of reference, the contained term being the whole of the sentence (51).

The inscrutability of reference, or what we will refer to as *weak* indeterminacy of translation, would then seem to be the thesis that a stimulus-response analysis of linguistic usage is insufficient to reveal ontological commitments. This is, we think, part of the thesis. But it is not all. For it would be a mistake to conclude that it follows that *we* can know, having a mastered a sophisticated language that includes all the machinery of individuation, what *we* are talking about, what objects *our* theories commit us to, but *not* what the Antorians are talking about, not what their theories commit them to. The inscrutability or indeterminacy in question applies also to ourselves and our own

73

theories. We know that 'rabbit' is a general term true of rabbits only by taking our own language and theories at face value. We could apply the technique of radical translation to our own language, each to our own idiolect, and discover that 'rabbit' can be reinterpreted as a term true of undetached rabbit parts. For each of us, the total set of sentences constituting our world theory would remain unchanged, or almost unchanged. Sentences we took to be true before the reinterpretation we would continue to take to be true. This seems to be taking us towards the view that what matters about our theories is the total set of sentences that constitutes them, the connections among those sentences, and the observation categoricals and observation sentences those theories imply. *Reference seems to be withering away.* In canonical notation, the notation of first order quantification theory, the sentences of our theory will have variables in referential position, and predicates that are taken to be true of the elements of the domain of the theory. But there is *no fact of the matter* about what the elements of that domain are.

But there is more to the inscrutability of reference or weak indeterminacy of translation. This thesis is not only about reference dropping out. It appears rather to be a more general doctrine, namely that for some range of sentences, including but not limited to sentences construed holophrastically, we can do sentence by sentence translations that result in the same or equivalent, near enough, translations of those sentences but treat of the component terms differently. 'Gavagai' is a special case of such sentences, a sentence with one component term. In the 'Gavagai' case, we can, on the basis of behavioral evidence, be assured that 'Gavagai' and 'Rabbit' are stimulus synonymous, near enough, while granting that the one component term of each ('gavagai' and 'rabbit') can be taken to refer to different kinds of things.[5] In the case of multi-word sentences, we can get the same–or distinct but equally acceptable and, for the purposes at hand, equivalent– translations of the sentences in question by divergent translation schemes, schemes that assign divergent roles to the constituent words. We have not yet reviewed this latter kind of case.

In "Ontological Relativity" Quine presents such a case. It involves particles in the Japanese language called "classifiers", which he notes can be explained "in either of two ways." It is easiest to here quote Quine at length:

> Commonly they (the classifiers) are explained as attaching to numerals, to form compound numerals of distinctive styles. Thus take the numeral for 5. If you attach one classifier to it

you get a style of "5" suitable for counting animals; if you attach a different classifier, you get a style of "5" suitable for counting slim things like pencils and chopsticks; and so on. But another way of viewing classifiers is to view them not as constituting part of the numeral, but as constituting part of the term–the term for "chopsticks" or "oxen" or whatever. On this view the classifier does the individuative job that is done in English by "sticks of" as applied to the mass term "wood," or "head of" as applied to the mass term "cattle."

What we have on either view is a Japanese phrase tantamount say to "five oxen," but consisting of three words; the first is in effect the neutral numeral "5," the second is a classifier of the animal kind, and the last corresponds in some fashion to "ox" (36).

Somewhat over simplified, the question is whether the third of the three Japanese words in question–the one corresponding in some fashion to 'ox'–functions as an adjective modifying the word for the numeral '5', or modifies the word for 'cattle', serving to transform that mass term into an individuative expression ('head of cattle'). Quine claims that

These are two very different ways of treating the third Japanese word; and the three-word phrase as a whole turns out all right in both cases only because of compensatory differences in our account of the second word, the classifier. (37.)

Not only will the three word phrase work whichever way it is treated, but

Between the two accounts of Japanese classifiers there is no question of right and wrong. The one account makes for more efficient translation into English; the other makes for more of a feeling for the Japanese idiom. Both fit all verbal behavior equally well. All whole sentences, and even component phrases like "five oxen," admit of the same net overall English translations on either account (37-38).

The overall translations come out the same, or nearly enough the same, either sentence by sentence or passage by passage. By 'same' or 'nearly enough the same' we mean that the alternative translation schemes do not give different accounts of what is going on, do not yield accounts such that we are inclined to count one true and the other false, either in total or in part. Intuitively, we recognize them as accounts of the same events or theories or whatever.

Quine thinks of both examples of indeterminacy (the one just discussed and that involving 'gavagai') as indeterminacy of reference because what is in question in both cases is what the reference of a term ('gavagai' and the third Japanese term) is (rabbits or rabbit stages... cattle, construing 'cattle' as a mass term, or each ox). In "Ontological Relativity" Quine remarks that

> Reference, extension, has been the firm thing; meaning, intension, the infirm. The indeterminacy of translation now confronting us [inscrutability of reference or weak indeterminacy of translation], however, cuts across extension and intension alike. The terms "rabbit," "undetached rabbit part," and "rabbit stage" differ not only in meaning; they are true of different things. Reference itself proves behaviorally inscrutable (35).

But despite the fact that this indeterminacy calls the firmness of extensionality into question, Quine does not seem to think it a serious indeterminacy. It arises from "the unsurprising reflection that divergent interpretations of the words in a sentence can so offset one another as to sustain an identical translation of the sentence as a whole" (1990b, 50).

The *strong indeterminacy of translation* is a different thesis. The weak thesis, just considered, leaves our theories intact; it calls into question the very coherence of the notion of reference, but does not require us to reevaluate our theories, to reassign truth-values (except perhaps within our theory of reference). In *Pursuit of Truth* Quine notes that

> The serious and controversial thesis of indeterminacy of translation is not that; it is rather the holophrastic thesis, which is stronger. It declares for divergences that remain unreconciled even at the level of the whole sentence, and are compensated for only by divergences in the translations of other whole sentences (50).

We think this strong indeterminacy of translation comes to the following. It is possible to construct alternative translation manuals for translating one language into another, say Japanese into English, such that for any fairly extended passage of the language being translated, the manuals will yield different translations, different to the point that in multiple instances a sentence of the language being translated will go over into a true sentence of English on one scheme and a false sentence of English on the other scheme. *Overall* the translation manuals will be deemed equally acceptable, for they make, overall, equally good sense of the behavior, linguistic and otherwise, of the speakers of the

76

language being translated. The difference between weak indeterminacy (indeterminacy of reference) and strong indeterminacy is that in the former, but not the latter, truth is preserved, sentence by sentence.

Where does this strong thesis come from and what is the evidence for it? We suspect that Quine takes the thesis to be, though strong and important, also obvious. It is an obvious consequence of Quine's notion of empirical content, of his willingness, indeed eagerness, to identify empirical meaning or content, in the only clear sense he can give to this notion, with experience (*i.e.*, the firings of sensory receptors). That is to say, Quine accepts the verificationist principle, but also maintains that the relationship with experience is, in the case of most sentences, spread across the network of theories (this is the thesis of holism). Strong indeterminacy of translation follows. Consider Quine's remarks in response to Roger Gibson in *The Philosophy of W.V. Quine*:

> Gibson cites Føllesdal's interesting observation that the indeterminacy of translation follows from holism and the verification theory of meaning. Føllesdal mistrusts this defense because of doubts about verificationism, and I gather that Gibson agrees. But I find it attractive. The statement of verificationism relevant to this purpose is that "evidence for the truth of a sentence is identical with the meaning of the sentence"; and I submit that if sentences in general had meanings, their meanings would be just that. It is only holism itself that tells us that in general they do not have them (155-156).

So, Quine is able to apply the above verificationist principle to his version of observation sentences and to observation categoricals, and he does so, identifying the meaning of these, or of their component sentences, with the relevant firings of sensory receptors. Holism precludes the assigning of meaning to individual sentences other than the above and ones like the above (*e.g.*, occasion sentences that are not themselves observation sentences but are best construed as being first learned holophrastically). As a result, translation is obviously indeterminate, for there will be multiple ways of translating sentences other than these special cases, all of which will yield equally plausible though non-equivalent bodies of theory to be attributed to the native speakers of the language. In *Pursuit of Truth* Quine remarks that

> What the indeterminacy of translation shows is that the notion of propositions as sentence meanings is untenable (102).

This suggests that indeterminacy of translation argues for holism. But we could as well say, as we did in earlier chapters, that the limits of verificationism (that it works only for a very limited range of sentences) itself argues for holism. This seems to be the argument of "Two Dogmas." Sentence meaning escapes us except for observation sentences and their kin, and therefore the notion of the proposition is in general untenable and for that reason translation is indeterminate. In the end, then, these notions, verificationism, holism, and sentence meaning being limited to observation sentences and their kin, are so interrelated that one can start from any one and get to the others. And the strong indeterminacy of translation follows from this cluster of concepts in the ways described above.

Why is the strong indeterminacy of translation thesis strong; why is it controversial and troubling? Suppose two field linguists have been studying the Antorians for a number of years, and that they have developed two non-equivalent manuals of translation. Suppose also that the Antorians have a society and culture much like ours (or such is our hypothesis), with theories of genetics and molecular biology and atomic physics whose sophistication seems on a par with ours. Suppose that the non-equivalent translation manuals our linguists have developed yield non-equivalent translations of Antorian genetics. Suppose also that our two field linguists (and their research teams–who have all gone bilingual) assure us that Antorian genetics seems as good as ours–as sophisticated, as predictive of future experience, and as well integrated into Antorian science as our genetics is into our science.

If Quine is right, the alternative translations of Antorian genetics will constitute, in English, two different and inconsistent theories of genetics. Our linguists will both grant that both cannot be accurate translations of Antorian genetics. We will see that both cannot be true. And the Antorians, whom we may presume have had their field linguists studying us, will produce multiple translation manuals for English to Antorian, with similar discrepancies. Overall, these manuals may well be equally acceptable. And there is *no fact of the matter* concerning which manuals are correct.

Finally, we might as well picture ourselves as becoming field linguists studying ourselves, and developing alternative translation manuals for English to English while being bound only by the requirement of preserving stimulus meaning and the canons of holism. We will develop distinct manuals of English to English translation, and they will attribute to us distinct, non-equivalent, theories. This is the strong indeterminacy of translation brought home.

Can we resolve the indeterminacy of translation, weak or strong? Weak indeterminacy, that concerning reference, can, in a sense, be resolved. In practice, the linguist resolves it by taking the extension of 'gavagai' to be rabbits, that is by imposing her own conceptual scheme on the native speakers of the language (1969b, 34). We can resolve it as it applies to our own idiolect and those of our neighbors, by "acquiescing in our mother tongue and taking its words at face value" (1969b, 49). But by so resolving it we have neither discovered, nor established, by fiat, a fact of the matter about reference. "[T]he inscrutability of reference is not the inscrutability of a fact; there is no fact of the matter" (1969b, 47).

What of the strong indeterminacy of translation? There is no fact of the matter here either, and the only apparent way of resolving the indeterminacy, by accepting one translation manual and rejecting all alternatives, has more arbitrariness about it than does accepting one's native tongue at face value, or so it seems. Strong indeterminacy holds that we could revise *any* significant sized body of theory, throwing out some sentences and compensating for those by adding others, and end up with a theory that, on holistic grounds, is as good as the first. But so construed the strong indeterminacy thesis comes to look very much like the underdetermination of theories thesis.

Underdetermination Revisited

We said near the beginning of this chapter, after laying out several ways in which theories can be seen as underdetermined, that we do not think Quine would demur that theories are not so underdetermined. But he might say that in that initial discussion of underdetermination we did not capture the underdetermination he is arguing for. In "Three Indeterminacies" Quine links the underdetermination of theories thesis with the thesis that "distinct global theories of the world may be empirically equivalent–that is, alike in empirical content." (13). And this suggests a relationship between the strong thesis of indeterminacy of translation and a strong version of underdetermination. Quine does not here seem to be talking about evolving theories, as we were in the beginning of this chapter, but rather of completed and global, or all encompassing, theories.

Note that when considered as a thesis about developing and specific theories, the thesis is not surprising. It is surely uncontroversial that in the history of science there are frequent points where the evidence available to date is consistent (or equally close to consistent) with, and equally supportive of, two or more alternative expansions of a developing theory. Researchers pursue one or another of the alternatives, for whatever pragmatic reasons, or more than one. Additional results rule out one or more of the alternatives. This is common fare, and holism can well accommodate it. Quine's claim is more than this. It is at least this: that no matter how far science advances there will always be, for science as a whole [see 1990b, 98], alternatives, alternatives equally supportable by available evidence. We tend to think of such alternative theories as equally supported but non-equivalent, as suggesting divergent lines of research. But this is not the kind of case Quine has in mind.

In *Word and Object* Quine writes

> ...*both* sorts of events [the behavior of molecules and of ordinary things] are less than determined by our surface irritations. This remains true even if we include all past, present, and future irritations of all the far-flung surfaces of mankind, and probably even if we throw in an in fact unachieved ideal organon of scientific method besides (22).

and

> ...we have no reason to suppose that man's surface irritations even unto eternity admit of any one systematization that is scientifically better or simpler than all possible others. It seems likelier... that countless alternative theories would be tied for first place (23).

In "Three Indeterminacies" Quine makes the argument implicit in these passages explicit. He there claims that "distinct global theories of the world, even logically incompatible ones, may be empirically equivalent–that is, alike in empirical content." They imply all the same observation categoricals but are logically incompatible. If this is a claim about what situation we will be in "at the end of science" we can object that it is not clear that science has an end. But whether science has an end or not, Quine need only respond that we seem to be able to imagine two global, logically incompatible theories that are empirically equivalent and continue to be so as time goes on–they continue to issue exactly the same predictions.

In "Three Indeterminacies" Quine gives an example, from Poincaré, of empirically equivalent theories neither of which can be reduced to the other.

> The one theory assumes infinite space in which the familiar rigid bodies move about without change in size. The other theory assumes a finite spherical space in which those bodies shrink uniformly as they move away from the center. The two are empirically equivalent (13).

They are equivalent, but they are hardly global theories. One requires an account of rigid bodies on which those bodies change size with relation to an identified spatial point, the other does not. Our broader theory of physics might lead us to pick one of these theories over the other.

But the larger point remains: Quine thinks there can be competing global theories that are empirically equivalent and also such that there is no non-arbitrary basis for preferring one to the other. This raises issues for the ascription of truth (which, if any, of such theories do we deem true), issues to which Quine devotes the last sections of *Pursuit of Truth*. But before taking up those issues we return to the question, asked at the outset of this section, of whether the strong indeterminacy of translation thesis is distinct from the underdetermination of theories thesis, when the latter is understood to envision global theories that are empirically equivalent but neither is reducible to the other.

Quine maintains these are distinct theses. In the concluding section of *Pursuit of Truth* he writes:

> There is an evident parallel between the empirical underdetermination of global science and the indeterminacy of translation. In both cases the totality of possible evidence is insufficient to clinch the system uniquely. But the indeterminacy of translation is additional to the other. If we settle upon one of the empirically equivalent systems of the world, however arbitrarily, we still have within it the indeterminacy of translation.
>
> Another distinctive point about the indeterminacy of translation is that it clearly has nothing to do with inaccessible facts and human limitations. Dispositions to observable behavior are all there is for semantics to be right or wrong about. In the case of systems of the world, on the other hand, one is prepared to believe that reality exceeds the scope of the human apparatus in unspecifiable ways (101).

And also

> What the indeterminacy of translation shows is that the notion of propositions as sentence meanings is untenable. What the empirical underdetermination of global science shows is that there are various defensible ways of conceiving the world (102).

It is on the basis of such passages that one wants to say that underdetermination is a thesis about evidence, indeterminacy a semantic thesis deriving from Quine's notion of meaning or the lack thereof. In cases of underdetermination, it makes sense to "picture to one's self" an alternative theory, with its posits, its notion of reality.

Not so with indeterminacy–where there is no fact of the matter. Surely Quine's claim that "In the case of systems of the world... one is prepared to believe that reality exceeds the scope of the human apparatus in unspecifiable ways" invites just this kind of thought experiment.

But while the indeterminacy of translation is clearly a semantic thesis, it is not entirely clear that the underdetermination of theories thesis is not also a semantic thesis–this because evidence and meaning coalesce for Quine via the verification principle. One wants to say that underdetermination is a consequence of holism, indeterminacy a consequence of meaning being limited, in the first instance, to stimulus meaning and therefore to observation sentences and their kin. But as we saw above, holism, the verification principle, and the impossibility of attaching meaning to separate sentences except for observation sentences and their kin, are pieces of a single fabric, pieces from which weak and strong indeterminacy of translation, as well as underdetermination of theories, all derive.

We certainly grant that underdetermination and weak indeterminacy (*i.e.*, inscrutability of reference) are distinct theses. One can take one's own language at face value and still be faced with the extreme underdetermination of theories we have just been discussing, as well as with the strong indeterminacy of translation. But this does not settle whether the latter two theses are really two.

Perhaps the answer is this: if we do take our own language at face value, take the extension of 'rabbit' to be rabbits, etc., then, from that internal perspective, we can entertain the question of whether "reality exceeds the scope of the human apparatus in unspecifiable ways"– because we will be taking posits both seriously and at face value, and wondering whether our posits due justice to reality. This seems to make sense. Strong indeterminacy of translation is, apparently, a separate thesis from this perspective–for we can become worried not only that our posits do not due justice to reality, but also, and separately, that radical translation, applied to our own theories, yields theories incompatible with ours but equally well supported by all available evidence. To hold on to our posits, at face value, we will have to say there is a fact of the matter in the one case, but not the other.

Truth

In the last pages of *Pursuit of Truth* Quine rehearses various ways of retaining the view that our accepted theories are true in the face of the global and enduring underdetermination of theories he has just sketched, where we have come to recognize that alternative theories to our overall theory of nature can be empirically equivalent to our accepted theory and to each other. In cases in which the competing theories are empirically equivalent, but one is far simpler or more natural, Quine is willing to appeal to these "coherence considerations" in deciding which theory to call 'true'. This speaks of an at least partial return to the strong holism of "Two Dogmas." Where the competing theories are equally natural and simple, Quine entertains two competing strategies, a *sectarian* one and an *ecumenical* one. The sectarian strategy is to retain the original theory and reject the concocted alternative theory. (This seems to presuppose that in such cases there will always be an original or going theory and that alternatives will always be "cooked up".) The ecumenical strategy is to count both theories, though logically incompatible, true. Quine opts for the sectarian strategy:

> The sectarian is no less capable than the ecumenist of appreciating the equal evidential claims of the two rival theories of the world. He can still be evenhanded with the cachet of warrantedness, if not of truth. Moreover he is as free as the ecumenist to oscillate between the two theories for the sake of added perspective from which to triangulate on problems. In his sectarian way he does deem the one theory true and the alien terms of the other theory meaningless, but only so long as he is entertaining the one theory rather than the other. He can readily shift the shoe to the other foot (100).

This is not a fully adequate resolution of the problem. But there are other suggestive remarks. One is this:

> The fantasy of irresolubly rival systems of the world is a thought experiment out beyond where linguistic usage has been crystallized by use (100).

This suggests that the extreme underdetermination thesis–that there can be rival theories of the world that are empirically equivalent (make all the same predictions of future experience) and incompatible–is empty, or at least has yet to be given full content. There remains the mundane kind of underdetermination of theories, also deriving from holism, that is far from empty and is clearly distinct from either indeterminacy thesis.

But an equally suggestive remark occurs in Quine's discussion of why he opts (though he does acknowledge some "vacillation") for the sectarian strategy. It seems to bring us back full circle to holism.

[When the two theories are equally simple and natural] we can no longer excuse this unequal treatment of [them] on the ground that our own is more elegant, but still we can plead that we have no higher access to truth than our evolving theory, however fallible (99).

This is strongly reminiscent of a passage in "Things and Their Place in Theories" in which Quine considers the implications of holism for truth.

...it is a confusion to suppose that we can stand aloof and recognize all the alternative ontologies as true in their several ways, all the envisaged worlds as real. It is a confusion of truth with evidential support. Truth is immanent, and there is no higher. We must speak from within a theory, albeit any of various (21-22).

Finally, there is the following passage from *Word and Object*, which suggests that we might say that the strong indeterminacy thesis emerges in the context of our engaging in epistemology–*i.e.*, in self-conscious theorizing about theory building–but still "from within," from within the bounds, the inescapable bounds, of the overall theory of nature we maintain and, via thought experiments, come to recognize as but one of possibly many empirically equivalent world theories.

Everything to which we concede existence is a posit from the standpoint of the description of the theory-building process, and simultaneously real from the standpoint of the theory that is being built. Nor let us look down on the standpoint of the theory as make-believe; for we can never do better than occupy the standpoint of some theory or other, the best we can muster at the time (22).

So the best we can do may be to take our own going theory at face value (settling the question of reference), dismiss the possibility of alternative global theories that are empirically equivalent to our going theory as currently empty, and accept the unsettling fact that there is no fact of the matter about radical translation.

Endnotes
[1] *"Three Indeterminacies,"* 1.

[2] See, for example, "Posits and Reality", 234.

[3] *In most, but not all, of his writings Quine uses 'underdetermined' rather than 'under-determined'. We have opted for the former usage.*

[4] Quine's "solution" to the problem of induction lies in his rejection of

naive inductivism–his emphasis on theory formation and holism, and perhaps in the positing of innate quality spaces that are to be explained by their evolutionary advantage.

[5] "It is philosophically interesting... that what is indeterminate in this artificial example is not just meaning, but extension; reference... Reference, extension, has been the firm thing; meaning, intension, the infirm. The indeterminacy of translation now confronting us, however, cuts across extension and intension alike. The terms "rabbit," "undetached rabbit part," and "rabbit stage" differ not only in meaning; they are true of different things. Reference itself proves behaviorally inscrutable" (1969b, 34-35).

8

Bringing Science to Bear

Better to discover how science is in fact developed and learned than to fabricate a fictitious structure to similar effect.

– W.V. Quine[1]

The Argument for Naturalizing Epistemology

"Epistemology Naturalized" and "Natural Kinds" were published in 1969, the third and fifth essays in *Ontological Relativity and Other Essays*. Although the essays launched what are today substantial research programs, Quine's arguments for and vision of naturalized epistemology remain deeply controversial in some philosophical quarters. In one sense, the controversy is not surprising. Viewed in light of the history of epistemology and the philosophy of science, Quine's suggestion that these enterprises be recognized and pursued as part of science ("as a chapter of psychology") is startling. It recommends against epistemology as generations of philosophers have pursued it (and as some continue to pursue it)–as a "first science" that is independent of science and the goal of which is to justify science. Quine argues, to the contrary, that epistemology is part and parcel of science, is science gone self-conscious.

But given Quine's views on topics we have already explored, the suggestion that traditional epistemology be abandoned in favor of self-conscious science is not startling at all. It follows close on the heels of Quine's recognition that the project Carnap undertook in *Aufbau* cannot be completed, and it reflects Quine's doubts (as early as 1936) that sentences of logic and mathematics are true by definition. Both figure

86

in the arguments of "Epistemology Naturalized." Moreover, Quine's rejection of the analytic/synthetic distinction makes the alleged non-empirical status of epistemology a non-starter. Finally, naturalized epistemology as Quine envisions it is a natural outcome of empiricism as Quine has sought to reconstitute it.

The opening pages of "Epistemology Naturalized" locate the sources of Quine's arguments for naturalizing epistemology in the failure, in the first half of the 20th century, to fulfill Hume's mandate to show that every truth can be accounted for either on grounds of logic (for logic and mathematics), or on grounds of sensory experience (for empirical truths). Quine's focus in this essay is, of course, the second project; but he begins by discussing the first. This enables him to later draw parallels between the failure of the first project (generally recognized by the time Quine published "Epistemology Naturalized"), and the failure he sees as inevitable (but not yet generally recognized) for the second. Commentators too often ignore these opening pages.

Quine notes that there were two focuses in studies into the foundations of mathematics. "Conceptual studies" were to show that the concepts of mathematics can be defined in the terms of logic. "Doctrinal studies" were to show that mathematical truths can be derived from the "obvious or at least potentially obvious... truths of logic" (70). The two projects are, of course, linked. If mathematical concepts are definable in the terms of logic, then the truths of mathematics are, in the end, truths of logic. If the latter are self-evident, so are the former.

The project failed, on both the conceptual and doctrinal sides, Quine notes, because it turned out that mathematics does not reduce to "logic proper," but "only to set theory" (70). This was a deep disappointment for two reasons.

> [T]he end truths, the axioms of set theory... have less obviousness and certainty to recommend them than do most of the mathematical theorems we would derive from then. Moreover, we know from Gödel's work that no consistent axiom system can cover mathematics even when we renounce self-evidence (70).

Thus, the reduction of mathematics to set theory does not "reveal the ground of mathematical knowledge," does not "show how mathematical certainty is possible" (70).

Against this background, Quine turns to efforts to identify the foundations of (recognizably) empirical science. Here there is also a conceptual project and a doctrinal project. The conceptual project, dating back to Hume, is to define sentences about physical bodies in terms of something directly linked to (or identical with) sensory experience. In this project, there has been progress. For Hume, bodies were to be identified with bundles of sense impressions, an approach Quine describes as "bold and simple." The subsequent shift from impressions to sentences as the bearers of empirical meaning (the second "milestone" of empiricism) shifted the focus of the conceptual project. The goal was now to show that sentences about bodies derive from or reduce to sentences about immediate sensory experience.

But, again it turned out that set theory was needed. And, as in studies into the foundations of mathematics, set theory compromised the conceptual project. Comparing the recourse to set theory with that of recognizing sentences as the bearers of meaning, Quine notes that

> The two resorts are very unequal in epistemological status. Contextual definition is unassailable. Sentences that have been given meaning as wholes are undeniably meaningful, and the use they make of their component terms is therefore meaningful, regardless of whether any translations are offered for those terms in isolation... Recourse to sets, on the other hand, is a drastic ontological move, a retreat from the austere ontology of impressions (73).

Quine's earlier discussion of studies into the foundations of mathematics is now brought to bear. The reason that recourse to set theory in studies of the foundations of empirical science was not generally recognized as a retreat from empiricism, Quine argues, is precisely the "deceptive hints of continuity between elementary logic and set theory" (73). These hints led Russell to be willing to define the conceptual project as that of accounting "for the external world as a logical construct of sense data," a project that Carnap's *Aufbau* came "nearest to executing" (74).

Even if Carnap's project had been successful, it would not have aided the *doctrinal* project. To show that the sentences of science can be so reconstructed does not show that these sentences "can be *proved* from observation sentences by logic and set theory" (74). "On the doctrinal side," Quine notes, "I do not see that we are farther along today than where Hume left us" (72).

Yet, Quine acknowledges that there were reasons to continue with the conceptual project, even in light of the abandonment of the doctrinal project and of the retreat that the recourse to set theory represented. One could still hope that the rational reconstruction of a sense datum language would "elicit" and "clarify" the sensory evidence for science, even if the steps between such evidence and scientific theories "fall short of certainty" (75). The reconstruction would contribute to understandings of how "all inculcation of meanings of words must rest ultimately on sensory evidence," for had Carnap or others succeeded, "the sensory content of discourse would stand forth explicitly" (75). It was not even necessary for Carnap to be able to demonstrate that the construction he arrived at was "the right one."

> The question would have had no point. He was seeking what he called a *rational reconstruction*. Any construction of physicalistic discourse in terms of sense experience, logic, and set theory would have been as satisfactory if it made the physicalistic discourse come out right. If there is one way there are many, but any would be a great achievement (75).

But, for reasons we earlier considered, Carnap did not succeed. In "Two Dogmas of Empiricism," Quine proposed holism as a counter-suggestion to applying verificationism. With that proposal the stage is set for Quine's suggestion in "Epistemology Naturalized" that the conceptual project be abandoned altogether.

> But why all this creative reconstruction, all this make-believe? The stimulation of his sensory receptors is all the evidence anybody has to go on, ultimately, in arriving at his picture of the world. Why not just see how this construction really proceeds? Why not settle for psychology? (75).

The turn to psychology (and Quine himself also appeals to linguistics and evolutionary theory) does represent a "surrender of the epistemological burden" to science; but this is appropriate given the abandonment of the doctrinal project.

> If the epistemologist's goal is validation of the grounds of empirical science, he defeats his purpose by using empirical science in the validation. However, such scruples against circularity have little point once we have stopped dreaming of deducing science from observations. If we are out simply to understand the link between observation and science, we are well advised to use any available information, including that provided by the very science whose link with observation we are seeking to understand (75-76).

Suppose, however, that we lower our sights on the conceptual side, seeking only to show that sentences of science can be *translated* into sentences involving sense data, logic, and set theory. If possible, such translation would further the Humean project by demonstrating "the essential innocence of physical concepts," showing them to be "theoretically superfluous." In so doing, "it would legitimize them–to whatever degree the concepts of set theory, logic, and observations are themselves legitimate" by demonstrating that "everything done with the one apparatus could in principle be done with the other" (76). The project might also retain a role for philosophy.

> If psychology itself could deliver a truly translational reduction of this kind, we should welcome it; but certainly it cannot, for certainly we did not grow up learning definitions of physicalistic language in terms of a prior language of set theory, logic, and observation (76).

The problem, Quine notes, is that Carnap's project did not succeed even in terms of translation. The point at which it becomes clear that Carnap's translation will not succeed, Quine argues, "comes where Carnap is explaining how to assign sense qualities in physical space and time" (76). In "Two Dogmas," we have seen, Quine argues that Carnap is unable to show how to translate a "statement of the form 'Quality q is at $x;y;z;t$' [a point instant]... into [his] initial language of sense data and logic" (40). Thus, Carnap is forced in subsequent writings to settle for "reduction forms," something far less than straightforward translation. In "Epistemology Naturalized," Quine notes that, rather than providing a way to eliminate the terms of one sentence by translating it into another, these forms

> do not in general give equivalences; they give implications. They explain a new term, if only partially, by specifying some sentences which are implied by sentences containing the term, and other sentences which imply sentences containing the term (77).

This is a far cry from the outcome that translation "of the sterner kind" would have generated. To give up the project of defining (via translation) physical concepts in terms of observation, logic, and set theory, is to give up "the last remaining advantage that we supposed rational reconstruction to have over straight psychology,"

> namely, the advantage of translational reduction. If all we hope for is a reconstruction that links science to experience in explicit ways short of translation, then it would seem more sensible to settle for psychology. Better to discover how science is in fact developed and learned than to fabricate a fictitious structure to similar effect (78).

As he did in "Two Dogmas," Quine suggests that the source of the failure of the various projects just summarized is that most sentences do not have their own empirical meaning. The problem is not that "the experiential implications of a typical statement about bodies are too complex for finite axiomatization, however lengthy," but

> that the typical statement about bodies has no fund of experiential implications it can call its own. A substantial mass of theory, taken together, will commonly have experiential implications; this is how we make predictions. We may not be able to explain why we arrive at theories which make successful predictions, but we do arrive at such theories (79).

Since most of the sentences to be reduced or translated do not have their own empirical meaning, if we persist in translation projects, we will need to focus on the "significantly inclusive portion" of a theory that has empirical meaning, axiomatizing "all the experiential difference that the truth of the theory would make" (79). This, Quine suggests, would be a "queer translation" because it would involve translating "the whole but none of its parts" and, indeed, perhaps 'translation' is not even the correct description. What we will have, in the end, might better be termed the "observational evidence for theories," their empirical meaning (79-80).

But we would do still better to give up translation projects all together. This is because, as we saw in the last chapter, the indeterminacy of translation plagues "even ordinary unphilosophical translation, such as from English into Arunta or Chinese." Here, Quine repeats the argument he offered in "Speaking of Objects" that "we can justify [the translation of sentences of English] into Arunta only together as a body," that there will be translations that will preserve the empirical implications of the theory we are translating (the observation sentences and observation categoricals it implies), and thus there will be no grounds for saying one is correct. That is, if holism holds, indeterminacy of translation follows for everything but observation sentences and their kin.

> If we recognize with Peirce that the meaning of a sentence turns purely on what would count as evidence for its truth, and if we recognize with Duhem that theoretical sentences have their evidence not as single sentences but only as larger bocks of theory, then the indeterminacy of translation of theoretical sentences follows. And most sentences, apart from observation sentences, are theoretical (81).

In the end, then, holism dictates the abandonment of the various conceptual projects to identify a foundation for science in sense data. In contrast to those who see "the irreducibility" involved as "the bankruptcy of epistemology," Quine suggests "it may be more useful to say rather that epistemology still goes on, though in a new setting and a clarified status." Epistemology "or something like it, simply falls into place as a chapter of psychology and hence of natural science" (82).

Epistemology in Its New Setting

What precisely is the new setting of epistemology? Although Quine mentions empirical psychology each time he suggests abandoning "the old epistemology," neither his own work subsequent to "Epistemology Naturalized," nor the balance of the essay, suggests that philosophers will or should abandon epistemological questions all together. Rather, both suggest "an interplay" between psychology (as well as all other relevant sciences) and "the new epistemology." Epistemology, engaged in by psychologists or philosophers, just is science gone self conscious; it is the use of the resources of science that marks the "conspicuous difference between old epistemology and epistemology in its new setting" (83). It is worth quoting at length two passages which suggest such interplay. In the first, Quine uses broad strokes to sketch the project of the new epistemology. Notice that his description presupposes a physicalist notion of experience, under-determination, and other aspects of empiricism as he has sought to reconstitute it.

> Epistemology, or something like it... studies a natural phenomenon, *viz.*, a physical human subject. This human subject is accorded a certain experimentally controlled input—certain patterns of irradiation in assorted frequencies, for instance–and in the fullness of time the subject delivers as output a description of the three-dimensional external world and its history. The relation between the meager input and the torrential output is a relation we are prompted to study for somewhat the same reasons that always prompted epistemology; namely, in order to see how evidence relates to theory, and in what ways one's theory of nature transcends any available evidence (83).

That the input accorded the species is meager relative to our output, and that the input consists in the firings of sensory receptors, are implications of the output (theories) we deliver in response to those firings. That is, psychology is itself part of the bridge we have built to explain and predict such firings.

> The old epistemology aspired to contain, in a sense, natural science; it would construct it somehow from sense data. Epistemology in its new setting, conversely, is contained in natural science, as a chapter of psychology. But the old containment remains valid too, in its way. We are studying how the human subject of our study posits bodies and projects his physics from his data, and we appreciate that our position in the world is just like his. Our very epistemological enterprise, therefore, and the psychology wherein it is a component chapter, and the whole of natural science wherein psychology is a component book–all this is our own construction or projection from stimulations like those we were meting out to our epistemological subject (83).

Thus, Quine concludes, "there is... reciprocal containment, though containment in different senses: epistemology in natural science and natural science in epistemology."

In the balance of "Epistemology Naturalized," Quine explores how using the resources of psychology might help clarify the notion of an observation sentence, and how such clarification will contribute to the conceptual and doctrinal projects of naturalized epistemology. Some hints are contained in the broad sketch of naturalized epistemology, earlier quoted. Notably absent from the project are experiences of which we are aware. This reflects Quine's view of the implications of empirical science (that sensory evidence just is firings of sensory receptors) and the kind of empirical investigations called for on the basis of this implication. Approaching observation sentences in terms of the firings of sensory receptors both dissolves some old philosophical questions and reflects the abandonment of the project to justify science. No longer concerned with the latter project, "awareness ceased to be demanded"; observation can be defined "in terms of the simulation of sensory receptors, let consciousness fall where it may" (84).

We have devoted considerable discussion in earlier chapters to Quine's notions of experience and observation sentences, and turn now to "Natural Kinds." Here, Quine engages in the kind of epistemology just outlined. "Natural Kinds" is a complex and substantial essay, and it warrants more extensive discussion than we can provide. We focus on the ways in which it exemplifies and clarifies naturalized epistemology. Its topics are two hallmarks of human reasoning–"our sorting of things into kinds" (116) and induction–the relationship between them, and what explains them. Each, in one sense, is a problem. On the one hand, it is an implication of research in psychology and linguistics that there is "nothing more basic to thought and language than our sense of similarity, our sorting of things into kinds" (160). Sorting by resemblance–in terms both "of a resemblance between the present circumstances and past circumstances" in which a word is used, and in terms of phonetic resemblance–is necessary to language learning. Moreover, induction itself depends on the first sort of sorting and "our tendency to expect similar causes to have similar effects" (116 117).

> A standard of similarity is in some sense innate. This point is not against empiricism; it is a commonplace of behavioral psychology... Without some prior spacing of qualities, we could never acquire a habit; all stimuli would be equally alike and equally different... Moreover, in this behavioral sense it can be said equally of other animals that they have an innate standard of similarity too. It is part of our animal birthright (123).

On the other hand, "the notion of similarity or kind," so basic to human thinking and induction, "is alien to logic and set theory" (121) and "characteristically animal in its lack of intellectual status" (123). Moreover, "the relation between similarity and kind is less clear and neat than could be wished" (121). Having spent considerable time in the essay to establish these several points, Quine's question is this:

> For me... the problem of induction is a problem about the world; a problem of how we, as we now are (by our present scientific lights), in a world we never made, should stand better than random or coin-tossing chances of coming out right, when we predict by inductions which are based on our innate, scientifically unjustified similarity standard (127).

The question, we have seen, presupposes results in several sciences which suggest innate quality spacing in both our own and other species. It also presupposes Quine's efforts, and those by Carnap, to make the notion of "kind" respectable by using logic and set theory. Quine takes these efforts to fail: "definition of similarity in terms of kind is halting, and definition of kind in terms of similarity is unknown" (121). Finally, Quine's version of the problem of induction reflects the results of science, and of naturalizing epistemology.

> It is reasonable that our quality space should match our neighbor's, we being birds of a feather; and so the general

94

trustworthiness of induction in the ostensive learning of words was a put-up job. To trust induction as a way of access to the truths of nature, on the other hand, is to suppose, more nearly, that our quality space matches that of the cosmos. The brute irrationality of our sense of similarity, its irrelevance to anything in logic and mathematics, offers little reason to expect that this is somehow in tune with the world–a world which, unlike language, we never made... Why should our subjective spacing of qualities have a special purchase on nature and a lien on the future? (125-26)

The answer Quine proposes is two fold. First he suggests that "Darwin's natural selection is a plausible partial explanation" (perhaps "almost explanation enough" (127)) for our innate quality spacing and our use of induction.

> If people's innate spacing of qualities is a gene-linked trait, then the spacing that has made for the most successful inductions will have tended to predominate through natural selection. Creatures inveterately wrong in their inductions have a pathetic but praise-worthy tendency to die before reproducing their kind (126).

What makes natural selection "perhaps enough of an explanation" is that it can also explain induction's "conspicuous failures" (127). Sorting by color, for example, seems endemic to the species and explicable in terms of its survival value (for example, it is useful for food-gathering). At the same time, our most serious theories of nature suggest that colors do "not qualify as kinds" and that the "distinctions that matter for basic physical theory are mostly independent of color contrasts" (127).

This sets the stage for the second part of Quine's answer.

> One's sense of similarity or one's system of kinds develops and changes and even turns multiple as one matures, making perhaps for increasingly dependable prediction. And at length standards of similarity set in which are geared to theoretical science. This... is a development away from the immediate, subjective, animal sense of similarity to the remoter objectivity of a similarity determined by scientific hypotheses and posits and constructs. Things are similar in the later or theoretical sense to the degree that they are interchangeable parts of the cosmic machine revealed by science (134).

Science both reveals innate similarity space and dispositions to induction, and explains them (via Darwin's theory of natural selection). At the same time, analyses of science's development and success, of the sort Quine here engages in, suggest that "things about [our] innate similarity sense that are helpful in one sphere [*e.g.*, color to food gathering] can be a hindrance in the other [the search by science for "more significant regularities"]" (128). As a result, we learn that

> Evidently natural selection has dealt with the conflict by endowing man doubly: with both a color-slanted quality space and the ingenuity to rise about it.
>
> He has risen above it by developing modified systems of kinds, hence modified similarity standards for scientific purposes. By the trial-and-error process of theorizing he has regrouped things into new kinds which prove to lend themselves to many inductions better than the old (128).

Indeed, Quine suggests, "we can take it as a very special mark of the maturity of a branch of science that it no longer needs an irreducible notion of similarity and kind" (138).

Thus, naturalized epistemology as Quine engages in it is both an explanatory and a normative enterprise. It can both explain and evaluate the innate dispositions science reveals, and assess the maturity of the specific sciences in light of our best going theories, "our theory of the world itself" (135), which suggest that we do well to move beyond the notions of similarity we have inherited. It is our going theory of nature which indicates that the development from innate similarity spacing to theoretical similarity is an advance, and that we might hope for the disappearance altogether of the notion of similarity in our most refined theory of nature. "The career of the similarity notion," Quine suggests, "is a paradigm of the evolution of unreason into science" (138). This is, of course, a normative assessment, an evaluation of both common-sense theorizing and scientific theorizing. It draws on knowledge provided by the sciences and simultaneously assesses scientific theorizing on the basis of that very same knowledge.

Thus, the epistemologist who engages in science gone self-conscious is, like everyone else, working from within our best going theory of nature, and using aspects of it to evaluate our progress in rebuilding the ship in which we are afloat.

Endnotes
[1] Epistemology Naturalized, 78.

Works Cited

Barrett, Robert B. and Roger F. Gibson 1990, *Perspectives on Quine.* Cambridge, MA: B. Blackwell.

Davidson, Donald and Jaakko Hintikka 1969, *Words and Objections: Essays on the Work of W.V. Quine.* Boston, MA: D. Reidel Publishing Company.

Duhem, Pierre 1954 (1991), *The Aim and Structure of Physical Theory.* Translated by Philip P. Wiener. Princeton, NJ: Princeton University Press.

Hahn, Edwin Lewis and Paul Arthur Schilpp 1987, *The Philosophy of W.V. Quine.* LaSalle, IL: Open Court.

Hume, David 1902 *Enquiries Concerning the Human Understanding and Concerning the Principles of Morals,* edited by Selby-Bigge (impression of 1961). London: Oxford University Press.

Quine, W.V. 1960, *Word and Object.* Cambridge, MA: MIT Press.

Quine, W.V. 1963, *From a Logical Point of View.* New York, NY: Harper & Row, second edition.

1963a, "On What There Is," in *From a Logical Point of View.*

1963b, "Two Dogmas of Empiricism," *in From a Logical Point of View.*

Quine, W.V. 1966, *The Ways of Paradox and Other Essays,* New York, NY: Random House.

1966a, "The Ways of Paradox," *in The Ways of Paradox and Other Essays.*

1966b, "Foundations of Mathematics," in *The Ways of Paradox and Other Essays.*

1966c, "Necessary Truth," in *The Ways of Paradox and Other Essays.*

1966d, "Truth by Convention," in *The Ways of Paradox and Other Essays.*

1966e, "On Mental Entities," in *The Ways of Paradox and Other Essays.*

1966f, "The Scope and Language of Science," in *The Ways of Paradox and Other Essays.*

1966g, "Posits and Reality," in *The Ways of Paradox and Other Essays.*

1966h, "Mr. Strawson on Logical Theory," in *The Ways of Paradox and Other Essays.*

Quine, W.V. 1969, *Ontological Relativity and Other Essays.* New York, NY: Columbia University Press.

1969a, "Speaking of Objects," in *Ontological Relativity and*

Other Essays.

1969b, "Ontological Relativity," in *Ontological Relativity and Other Essays.*

1969c, "Epistemology Naturalized," in *Ontological Relativity and Other Essays.*

1969d, "Natural Kinds," in *Ontological Relativity and Other Essays.*

Quine, W.V. 1970, "Grades of Theoreticity," in *Experience & Theory,* eds. L. Foster, and J.W. Swanson, 1970. Cambridge, MA: MIT Press.

Quine, W.V. 1978, "Facts of the Matter," in *Essays on the Philosophy of W.V. Quine,* eds. R.W. Shahan and C. Swoyer, 1978. Norman: The University of Oklahoma Press.

Quine, W.V. 1981, *Theories and Things.* Cambridge, MA: Harvard University Press.

1981a, "Things and Their Place in Theories," in *Theories and Things.*

1981b, "Empirical Content," in *Theories and Things.*

1981c, "On the Very Idea of a Third Dogma," in *Theories and Things.*

1981d, "On the Nature of Moral Values," in *Theories and Things.*

1981e, "Five milestones of Empiricism," in *Theories and Things.*

1981f, "On Austin's Method," in *Theories and Things.*

1981g, "Responses," in *Theories and Things.*

1981h, "The Times Atlas," in *Theories and Things.*

Quine, W.V. 1985, *The Time of My Life.* Cambridge, MA: MIT Press.

Quine, W.V. 1987a, *Quiddities: An Intermittently Philosophical Dictionary.* Cambridge, MA: Harvard University Press.

Quine, W.V. 1987b, "Autobiography of W.V. Quine," in *The Philosophy of W.V. Quine.*

Quine, W.V. 1990a, "Three Indeterminacies," in *Perspectives on Quine.*

Quine, W.V. 1990b, *Pursuit of Truth.* Cambridge, MA: Harvard University Press.